TOEIC is a registered trademark of ETS.
This product is not endorsed or approved by ETS.   L&R means LISTENING AND READING.

# STRATEGIC PRACTICE FOR THE TOEIC® L & R TEST

## 600点を目指すTOEIC® L&R TEST演習

**Emiko Matsumoto / Kentaro Nishii / Sam Little**

SANSHUSHA

# はじめに

## ❖ 本書で学ぶ皆さんへ ❖

　TOEIC® の勉強は、決して文法の勉強だけ、単語暗記だけではありません。TOEIC® で出てくる英語はビジネスや、日常生活で使われる英語です。英語は生きたコミュニケーションや会話の中で使用されます。

　皆さんはいろいろな社会の中で生きています。「社会」というとなんだか立派なものに聞こえるかもしれませんが、皆さんが毎日顔を合わせる家族や、学校の友達と会うクラスや、クラブ、サークル活動も社会の一つです。

　皆さんが発した言葉の一つひとつが聞いている相手や、その会話を聞いているほかの人にも影響を与え、皆さんの住む世界が毎日少しずつ変化していくのです。

　皆さんが毎日、感じていることは周りのみんなも同じように感じているのでしょうか。例えば、見えるもので言うと、教室の窓から見える木々の葉の色が、緑に見えるのか、黄緑に見えるのか、それを深緑と呼ぶ人がいるのか。その葉の色を、隣の校舎の窓から見ている人が同じように感じるかどうか。それは誰にもわからないし、おそらく少しずつ違っているのでしょう。

　また、聞こえるものでは、空港から離陸する旅客機の音を想像してみてください。それを騒音と感じるのか、心地よい音楽のようだと感じるのか、悲しいと感じるのか、感動して聞いているのかは、あなたがいる場所、状況、誰と一緒にいるのかによって変化しますよね。

　ある日、あなたは大切な友達と言い争いをしてしまいました。相手とうまく仲直りができずに、別れてしまったかもしれません。あなたは
「相手に嫌われたに違いない」
「相手との人間関係は終わってしまった」
　とひどく傷ついてしまいました。
でも、相手はどう思っているのでしょう。

あなたが感じていることと、相手が感じていることは、きっと少しだけ違うはずです。しかも、少し時間が経つと、あなたが感じていること、相手が感じていることは、お互いに、良い方向に変化するでしょう。コミュニケーションや会話って生き物なのです。

　もし、言い争いをしてしまった相手と、少しでも良い関係を築きたいのなら、明日、思い切って、「君はすごいね」と話しかけてみましょう。相手はすぐには素直になれなくても、きっとあなたの言葉が化学変化を起こし、数日で関係を修復できるはずです。

　何かに行き詰まったら、いつまでも同じ思考回路をグルグルまわるのはやめて、あなたから新しいパターンのコミュニケーションを始めてみましょう。

　母国語が日本語の私にとって、日本語はとても美しく、感情移入がしやすい言葉です。

　しかし、行き詰まってしまった時、私は英語を勉強してきたこと、英語を聴いたり読んだりできることを、ありがたいと思います。なぜなら、英語で問題解決のヒントを得ることもできるし、自分が英語の世界からものを見て、考えることができるからです。

　英語の勉強は一見、単純なことの積み重ねに見えるかもしれません。でも、その積み重ねのおかげで新しい自分に出会うことができるのなら、しばらくの間、英語学習を続けてみませんか。TOEIC® 学習によって、皆さんがスコアアップされ、その向こうに幸せな将来があることを心よりお祈りしています。

著者代表　松本恵美子

## 本書の特長

　本書は TOEIC® 初心者から中級者のためのテキストです。TOEIC® LISTENING AND READING TEST のスコアアップに必要な基礎力と実力を身につけることを目的に編集されました。2016 年から導入されている現在のテスト形式に対応しています。1 ユニットで全てのパートの練習をすることができるように組み立てられており、授業進度に応じて、1 ユニット進むのに 1 コマ、もしくは 2 コマ以上の時間をかけてもよいでしょう。授業内の短時間で TOEIC® 形式の問題に慣れ、解答のコツを身につけながら実践問題に親しむことができます。

　特長として次の 4 つを挙げることができます。

## 本書の構成と特長

① 全 15 ユニット構成、Unit 1 〜 14 の各ユニットの問題数は全 25 問

　　各ユニット、Part 1（2 問）、Part 2（4 問）、Part 3（3 問）、Part 4（3 問）、Part 5（4 問）、Part 6（4 問）、Part 7（5 問）の全 25 問となっており、1 つのユニットで Part 1 〜 Part 7 までの実践問題が学習できます。

② Unit 1 〜 14 の各ユニットの始めには Vocabulary Check

　　そのユニットに関連した単語を最初に学習することができます（12 語）。

③ Unit 15 はミニテストで問題数は全 35 問

　　ミニテストは Part 1（4 問）、Part 2（10 問）、Part 3（3 問）、Part 4（3 問）、Part 5（6 問）、Part 6（4 問）、Part 7（5 問）の全 35 問となっています。

④ 教授用資料としてリスニング・スクリプトの穴埋め問題、単語テスト

　　授業用の資料として、リスニングの全スクリプトと、その穴埋め問題、単語テストを用意しています。

　本書の作成にあたり、Unit 1 〜 Unit 14 の Vocabulary Check、Unit 1 〜 Unit 15 の Part1、Part2、Part3、Part5 とその解説、全体の監修を松本が、Unit 1 〜 Unit 15 の Part 4、Part 6 と Part 7 とその解説を西井が、全文の英文校閲を Little が担当しました。本書を効果的に活用され、TOEIC® スコアアップのための英語力を身につけられることを心より祈っております。

# Contents

**音声ダウンロード＆ストリーミングサービス（無料）のご案内**

https://www.sanshusha.co.jp/text/onsei/isbn/9784384335200/

本書の音声データは、上記アドレスよりダウンロードおよびストリーミング再生ができます。ぜひご利用ください。

UNIT **1**
Restaurant

## Vocabulary Check!

Choose an appropriate translation for the following words.

🔊 01

1. sponsorship (　) 2. whisk (　) 3. inflammation (　)

4. forecast (　) 5. rehabilitation (　) 6. appetizer (　)

7. flexible (　) 8. patronage (　) 9. organic (　)

10. acute (　) 11. ingredient (　) 12. mayor (　)

---

a. リハビリテーション　　b. 予報　　c. 前菜　　d. 後援、賛助

e. 有機的　　f. 融通のきく　　g. 炎症　　h. 泡だて器

i. 材料、内容物　　j. 市長　　k. 急性の

l. スポンサーであること、資金提供

# 🎧 Listening Section

## Part 1  Photographs

**Strategy for Part 1** ［写真描写問題の解き方］

**人物 1 人の写真 ①**

　人物が 1 人だけ写っている写真、または 1 人の人物にフォーカスを当てている場合は、選択肢の主語はすべて同じ語（He, She, The man, A woman など）であることが多いです。このユニットでは、写真の人物が 1 人の場合に主語がすべて同じかどうか、確認してみましょう。

1.

Ⓐ Ⓑ Ⓒ Ⓓ

2.　🔊 02

Ⓐ Ⓑ Ⓒ Ⓓ

## Part 2  Question-Response

**Strategy for Part 2** ［応答問題の解き方］

**疑問詞で始まる疑問文 ①　Where, Who, When**

　Part 2 の設問の半分以上は 5 W 1 H の疑問詞で始まる疑問文です。まず、文頭の What / When / Where / Who / Why / How を聞き取り、それを忘れないように記憶しておきましょう。

🔊 03

3.　Mark your answer on your answer sheet.　　Ⓐ Ⓑ Ⓒ

4.　Mark your answer on your answer sheet.　　Ⓐ Ⓑ Ⓒ

5.　Mark your answer on your answer sheet.　　Ⓐ Ⓑ Ⓒ

6.　Mark your answer on your answer sheet.　　Ⓐ Ⓑ Ⓒ

## Part 3  Conversations

**Strategy for Part 3 ［会話問題の解き方］**

**Part 3 で必要な能力とは… ①**

　Part 3 では男女 2 人または 3 人の会話に続いて設問 3 問を聞き、それぞれ 4 つの選択肢を読んで解答します。漫然と音声を聞くのではなく、男性、女性、それぞれの状況、立場をきちんと理解して正解を選ぶ、という会話のバックグラウンドを想像する力が必要です。

Questions 7-9　　　　　　　　　　　　　　　　　　🔊 04

7.　What is the conversation mainly about?

　(A) The weather forecast

　(B) The restaurant menu

　(C) The man's favorite drink

　(D) The man's health

8.　How did the man recover from his illness?

　(A) Through surgical therapy

　(B) By being hospitalized

　(C) By avoiding a certain kind of food

　(D) Through rehabilitation

9.　What does the man decide to do?

　(A) He won't drink another glass of wine.

　(B) He will order a bottle.

　(C) He will accept the woman's suggestion.

　(D) He won't drink with her anymore.

## Part 4  Talks

Questions 10-12                                                    🔊 05

**10.** What happened at La Seine 10 years ago?

(A) It received a prize.

(B) It was newly opened.

(C) Emily Jordan was promoted.

(D) Joseph Kent joined the staff.

**11.** According to the speaker, what was Ms. Jordan interested in?

(A) Finding local ingredients

(B) Growing organic vegetables

(C) Increasing profits

(D) Creating new recipes

**12.** Who is Eric Bennett?

(A) A chef

(B) A manager

(C) A food supplier

(D) A business owner

**Part 5** Incomplete Sentences

**Strategy for Part 5** ［短文穴埋め問題の解き方］

動詞の形問題 ① 「主語」と「述語動詞」を探そう

　短文穴埋め問題では、問題の種類を、「動詞の形」に関する問題、「品詞」の問題、「文法」問題、「語彙」問題の４つに分類することができます。

　選択肢を見て、同じ動詞の様々な形が並んでいたら、「動詞の形」問題だと判断しましょう。その場合、まず、**「主語」**と**「動詞」**を探しましょう。主語と動詞があることを確認したら、文の意味よりも空所に入る「時制」や、「３単現の s はつくのか、つかないのか」について考えて解答します。

13. The shop manager ------- absent from the staff meeting yesterday because of an urgent order from a customer.

    (A) is          (B) was          (C) has          (D) will be

14. People around me in my office ------- a lot of junk food.

    (A) is eating      (B) eating      (C) eat      (D) eats

15. Five years ------- since my son went over to Paris in order to study French cuisine.

    (A) passed      (B) was      (C) are passed      (D) have passed

16. My boss is always ------- about the food in our company's cafeteria.

    (A) complain      (B) complaining      (C) complained      (D) being complained

## Part 6  Text Completion

### Strategy for Part 6 ［長文穴埋め問題の解き方］

**Part 5 に続く 2 つ目の穴埋めパート**

Part 6 は「長文穴埋め問題」です。Part 5 のような 1 つの文ではなく、複数の文で構成される 1 つの文書で 4 か所の空所を埋めていきます。

しかし「長文」と言っても、1 文書は 100 語前後、実は**トピックを 1 つしか書けないほどの長さ**でしかありません（＝たいてい 1 段落です）。また、すべて穴埋め問題ですが、複数の文で構成されているので、空所のある文だけでなく、その前後の文を読むことも必要となります。

**Part 5 と Part 6** を合わせて **20 分**程で手際よく解けるようになると、Part 7 に使える時間が増え、**リーディング後半の問題からも正解を拾うことができるようになり**、それだけでスコア・アップにつながる人も少なくありません。

Questions 17-20 refer to the following message.

Our Chef, Double Awarded!

We are ------- to let our loyal customers know that this year's Best Chef Award went
    **17.**
to one of our finest chefs, Linda Wood, at the Preston Culinary Contest.

The award ceremony ------- in the city hall on August 29. Then, the mayor, Mike
    **18.**
Bloom, made a surprising announcement in his complimentary speech. Can you
believe that the city decided to ------- her the Honorary Citizen Award?
    **19.**

Remember, from September 8 to 11, she will recreate the same dishes herself as
she served at the contest, for just 10 customers every day. -------.
    **20.**

*Mario Ferrini*
Manager, Cavatore Restaurant

**17.** (A) delightful     (B) delighted     (C) delight     (D) delightfully

**18.** (A) was held     (B) held     (C) will be held     (D) will hold

**19.** (A) bring     (B) grant     (C) present     (D) contribute

**20.** (A) You may want to ask the staff nearby about her schedule.
     (B) Please don't miss this chance to enjoy the taste of our local star.
     (C) Now, we will start serving them when you are ready at table.
     (D) Also, her recipes will be available on our Web site on the same day.

**Strategy for Part 7** ［読解問題の解き方］

**Part 7 の全体像と時間配分**

　TOEIC L&R TEST リーディングセクション最後の Part 7 は「読解問題」で、パッセージ（文書）が計 15 個、54 問から成っています。まず、2 〜 4 問の設問がついた「シングル・パッセージ（1 文書）」が 10 セット（設問は 147 番〜 175 番まで 29 問）、次に 5 問の設問がついた「ダブル・パッセージ（2 文書）」が 2 セット（設問は 176 番〜 185 番まで 10 問）、最後に 5 問の設問がついた「トリプル・パッセージ（3 文書）」が 3 セット（設問は 186 番〜 200 番まで 15 問）並びます。**Part 7 全体で、約 55 分以上の時間を使えるように練習しましょう。**リーディングセクションで最も大切なことは**「時間管理」**です。

Questions 21-25 refer to the following letter.

---

17 April

Dear Mr. Rosenberg,

I am writing in response to your invitation to the grand-reopening of your restaurant with much gratitude. It would be my great pleasure to attend the reception as a guest speaker.

— [1] — I'd definitely like to help them prepare for the party dishes. However, I am afraid to tell you that I will be unavailable in the evening on the day, due to a business trip. — [2] —. Therefore, I was wondering if one of the chefs from your restaurant could help the students cook in the evening. I am sure cooking with the students will be a very rewarding experience for your chefs, too.

— [3] —. As for the party preparation, I would like to make a suggestion. — [4] —. I once read an article of yours in the local newspaper where you emphasized how this town is blessed to be so close to the sea. So, why don't you use as many locally caught ingredients as you can? I hope this will make the guests and the students more aware of the importance of the fishing industry in our town.
Thank you very much again for inviting me to this wonderful event. I look forward to seeing you and your reborn restaurant soon.

Sincerely,
Anne Purcell
Chief Instructor
Swindon Culinary School

---

21. Why is Ms. Purcell writing to Mr. Rosenberg?
    (A) To inform him of her absence from preparation
    (B) To invite him to her school ceremony
    (C) To ask him about the timetable of the event
    (D) To request him to change the venue

22. What is suggested about the party?
    (A) Its schedule is flexible.
    (B) Its venue will be opened in the evening.
    (C) Some students are invited as guests.
    (D) Some fish dishes will be served.

23. What is indicated about Ms. Purcell?
    (A) She used to work for the restaurant.
    (B) She is very interested in the event.
    (C) She will be taking a vacation.
    (D) She will launch a new business.

24. What does Ms. Purcell suggest doing for the event?
    (A) Advertising the event in the paper
    (B) Asking local companies for sponsorship
    (C) Using food caught nearby
    (D) Inviting the local residents

25. In which of the positions marked [1], [2], [3], and [4] does the following sentence best belong?

    "Furthermore, I appreciate your wonderful idea of letting our students make some of the dishes for the dinner party themselves."

    (A) [1]            (B) [2]            (C) [3]            (D) [4]

UNIT **2**
**Sightseeing**

## Vocabulary Check!

Choose an appropriate translation for the following words. 🔊 06

| | | |
|---|---|---|
| 1. presumably ( ) | 2. regular ( ) | 3. exhibition ( ) |
| 4. incur ( ) | 5. invoice ( ) | 6. aquarium ( ) |
| 7. itinerary ( ) | 8. splendid ( ) | 9. exempt ( ) |
| 10. vehicle ( ) | 11. allocate ( ) | 12. spacious ( ) |

| | | | |
|---|---|---|---|
| a. 乗り物 | b. 割り当てる | c. 広々とした | d. 免除する |
| e. おそらく | f. 展示 | g. 計算書 | h. 水族館 |
| i. 旅行日程 | j. すばらしい | k. 定期の | l. こうむる |

## 🎧 Listening Section

### Part 1  Photographs

**Strategy for Part 1**［写真描写問題の解き方］

**複数人物の写真 ①**

　複数人物が写真に写っている場合、主語を表す表現が写真と一致しているか確認しましょう。複数人物が同じ行動をしていて、それを描写している選択肢では、主語を They, People, Customers, Workers などで表していて、動詞部分で共通動作を表しているものが正解の場合が多いです。

**1.**

Ⓐ Ⓑ Ⓒ Ⓓ

**2.**　　🔊 07

Ⓐ Ⓑ Ⓒ Ⓓ

### Part 2  Question-Response

**Strategy for Part 2**［応答問題の解き方］

**疑問詞で始まる疑問文 ②　Where, Who, When**

　例えば、疑問文が Where で始まったら、「Where, Where, Where …（どこ？）」のように、頭の中でその疑問詞を繰り返して残しておきます。「場所」を聞かれていることを意識し、選択肢 (A)(B)(C) を聞き終わるまで忘れないように練習してみましょう。

🔊 08

**3.**　Mark your answer on your answer sheet.　　Ⓐ Ⓑ Ⓒ

**4.**　Mark your answer on your answer sheet.　　Ⓐ Ⓑ Ⓒ

**5.**　Mark your answer on your answer sheet.　　Ⓐ Ⓑ Ⓒ

**6.**　Mark your answer on your answer sheet.　　Ⓐ Ⓑ Ⓒ

## Part 3 Conversations

**Strategy for Part 3** ［会話問題の解き方］

**Part 3 で必要な能力とは… ②**

　Part 3 では、会話文を聞き、登場人物のバックグラウンドを瞬時に理解する能力とともに、設問、選択肢を一瞬で読み取る短文速読力も必要とされます。それには単語力や、主語、動詞、目的語の関係を誤解しないような、構文を見極める力も必要です。会話文の音声が流れる前、つまり Part 3 のディレクションが流れている間に設問と選択肢を読んでおきましょう。

Questions 7-9　　　　　　　　　　　　　　　🔊 09

7.　Where is the shuttle bus heading to?

(A) To the hot spring

(B) To the platform

(C) To the hotel

(D) To the station

8.　What does the woman want to see?

(A) A market

(B) An art museum

(C) A bridge

(D) Some beautiful scenery

9.　How long does it take from the fish market to her destination?

(A) 10 minutes

(B) 12 minutes

(C) 20 minutes

(D) 30 minutes

## Part 4  Talks

**Strategy for Part 4** ［説明文問題の解き方］

**各種トークの「展開」はほぼ決まっている！①**

　Part 4 に登場するトークの種類に、**「ツアー案内（tour information）」** があります。話し手（the speaker）はガイド（案内人）で、場所は博物館、美術館、工場などの「室内系」や、自然公園などの「野外系」です。

　ツアー開始前やツアー中に、**その日の予定、注意点などを、順を追って説明**する、比較的聞きやすい種類のトークです。皆さんもそのガイドツアーの参加者になったつもりで聞いてみてください。きっとトークへの集中力が高まることでしょう。

Questions 10-12　　🔊 10

**10.** Where is the talk most likely taking place?

(A) In a building

(B) In a parking lot

(C) On a beach

(D) On a street

**11.** What did the listeners receive at the entrance?

(A) A bus ticket

(B) A map book

(C) A leaflet

(D) An itinerary

**12.** What are the listeners advised to do after the tour?

(A) Go to the bus stop

(B) Shop at the store

(C) Stay in the lobby

(D) Check their belongings

## Part 5　Incomplete Sentences

13. Kevin ------- four days a week at the travel agency nearby.

    (A) works　　　　(B) working　　　　(C) have worked　　　(D) work

14. Although I had my portable light serviced, it still turns off by -------.

    (A) them　　　　(B) themselves　　　(C) it　　　　　　　(D) itself

15. My client told me that he would get to the airport at about two o'clock. I'll call you when he -------.

    (A) will come　　(B) come　　　　　(C) comes　　　　　(D) came

16. Dr. Hann ------- to find a new remedy for me for several weeks.

    (A) try　　　　　(B) is trying　　　　(C) was tried　　　(D) has been trying

## Part 6　Text Completion

Questions 17-20 refer to the following e-mail.

To: Kuniko Takahashi <k.takahashi@tb-moriya.or.jp >
From: Alberto Santiago <asantiago@ecotech.co.au>
Date: 17 April
Subject: Re: Invitation

Dear Ms. Takahashi,

On behalf of Ecotech Corporation, I am replying to you to thank you for inviting my company to the Morita City Tourism Exhibition this year. It was a great shame that we missed ------ it due to our scheduling conflict last year. ------.
      **17.**                                              **18.**

------ it is wonderful to hear that you will ------ have the most companies and
  **19.**                                    **20.** organizations ever this year, I am a little concerned about whether we can secure a booth at the venue. We would be grateful if you could reserve one for us, although you may have already received many applications from overseas.

I look forward to hearing from you soon.

Best regards,
Alberto Santiago
Senior manager, International Section, Ecotech Corporation

17. (A) attending      (B) attendance      (C) attended      (D) attendant

18. (A) By contrast, the number of tourists has decreased.
    (B) As a result, we decided to hold a conference next year.
    (C) However, there are no major changes to our schedule so far.
    (D) Therefore, we are delighted to accept your offer this time.

19. (A) Even if      (B) While      (C) Additionally      (D) Provided that

20. (A) exclusively      (B) quarterly      (C) promptly      (D) presumably

## Part 7  Single Passages / Multiple Passages

**Strategy for Part 7 ［読解問題の解き方］**

**設問のタイプ**

　Part 7 の設問は、下記のように、いくつかの決まった種類があります。この**「設問のタイプ」を意識して解く練習**をしていくと、一見様々なことをたずねているように見える各設問のイメージが、次第にはっきりとしてきます。さらに、「文書のどの辺りにヒントが出ているか」「選択肢は具体的か、抽象化されているか」「時間が足りなくなった場合、どのような問題は避けた方がよいのか」など、様々な気づきがあるはずです。

　Part 7 では**「読む力」**と**「解く（選択肢を選ぶ）力」**の両方が要求されます。2 つの力をバランスよく鍛えていきましょう。

　　1. 文書の目的・概要を問うタイプ　　　2. 文書の詳細情報を問うタイプ
　　3. 選択肢を文書と照らし合わせるタイプ　4. あてはまらない選択肢を選ぶタイプ
　　5. 書き手の意図を推測するタイプ　　　6. 単語の意味を問うタイプ
　　7. 文が入る位置を問うタイプ

Questions 21-25 refer to the following e-mail.

| To: | William Fielder <william.field@t-net.com> |
|---|---|
| From: | Linda Harwood <lharwood@lakelandtravel.co.ca> |
| Date: | May 24 |
| Subject: | Order #7795 |

Dear Mr. Fielder:

Thank you very much for booking your tour with Lakeland Travel Online. Before confirming the reservation you made on May 21, we would like to provide you with some additional information.

First, why don't you upgrade your hotel room and the seat on your flight? There are still a few more spacious rooms and some first-class seats available and it may be a good chance to make your travel more comfortable.

Next, there has been a change to your tour schedules. Cruising to Mora Island on Day 4 has been moved to Day 5, when you were supposed to have some free time on the beach, because all the ferry seats for the original day are sold out. Accordingly, you now have some free time on Day 4, we would like to introduce some excursion ideas for the day. Please click on the link 'Optional Tours' for more details on the Web site.

If you find the above interesting, please log-in to our Web site no later than May 28 and open the 'My Itinerary' tab to update your booking. We will check and confirm your final booking status on the next day.

Then, you will immediately receive the invoice online. Your full payment must be made within two business days from receiving it. Please note that any promotional codes are invalid during this busy season. Also, if you cancel the tour after your payment, an extra fee of 20 percent of the total amount will be incurred. We will send you the airline ticket by e-mail after we have confirmed your payment.

Should you have any further inquiries, please do not hesitate to contact us.

Best regards,
Linda Harwood
Customer Support
Lakeland Travel Ltd.

21. What is the purpose of the e-mail?
    (A) To cancel a reservation          (B) To make some suggestions
    (C) To confirm a booking             (D) To send some documents

22. What will Mr. Fielder receive after his payment?
    (A) An itinerary                     (B) An flight ticket
    (C) A receipt                        (D) An invoice

23. When is the payment able to be made?
    (A) May 21        (B) May 24        (C) May 27        (D) May 30

24. The word "incurred" in paragraph 5, line 4, is closest in meaning to
    (A) refunded      (B) discounted     (C) charged       (D) exempted

25. What is suggested about Lakeland Travel Ltd.?
    (A) It issues promotional codes available to use at any time.
    (B) It has some branches in other countries.
    (C) It offers both domestic and overseas travel plans.
    (D) It allocates a personal account to each customer.

UNIT **3**

# Business / Technology

## Vocabulary Check!

Choose an appropriate translation for the following words.  🔊 11

| | | |
|---|---|---|
| **1.** sufficient (   ) | **2.** malfunction (   ) | **3.** cupboard (   ) |
| **4.** shipment (   ) | **5.** book (   ) | **6.** deposit (   ) |
| **7.** appliance (   ) | **8.** recommend (   ) | **9.** extension (   ) |
| **10.** suspend (   ) | **11.** protective (   ) | **12.** equip (   ) |

| | | | |
|---|---|---|---|
| a. 予約する | b. 保護の | c. 推薦する | d. 備え付ける |
| e. 器具、装置 | f. 出荷 | g. 異常 | h. 十分な |
| i. 食器棚 | j. 入金、預金する | k. 吊るす | l. 延長 |

## 🎧 Listening Section

### Part 1  Photographs

**Strategy for Part 1 ［写真描写問題の解き方］**

**複数人物の写真 ②**

　複数人物が写真に写っていて、同じ行動をしていても、主語は They, People, Customers, Workers などではなく、周辺のものや、主語が注目したり（monitor, paper など）、身につけたり（uniform, gear など）しているものを主語とした文が選択肢となる場合もあります。

**1.**　　　　　　　　　　　　　　　　**2.**　　　　　　　　　　　🔊 12

Ⓐ Ⓑ Ⓒ Ⓓ　　　　　　　　　　Ⓐ Ⓑ Ⓒ Ⓓ

### Part 2  Question-Response

**Strategy for Part 2 ［応答問題の解き方］**

**疑問詞で始まる疑問文 ③　What, How, Which**

　How で始まる疑問文は「〜どうですか？」の意味だけではなく、そのあとに続く語によって、How many 〜, How much 〜, How long 〜, How far 〜 など、数や、量、金額、長さ、遠さなどを聞いています。一度マスターすれば、次に出てきた際にイメージしやすいでしょう。

🔊 13

**3.**　Mark your answer on your answer sheet.　　Ⓐ Ⓑ Ⓒ

**4.**　Mark your answer on your answer sheet.　　Ⓐ Ⓑ Ⓒ

**5.**　Mark your answer on your answer sheet.　　Ⓐ Ⓑ Ⓒ

**6.**　Mark your answer on your answer sheet.　　Ⓐ Ⓑ Ⓒ

---

**Strategy for Part 3** ［会話問題の解き方］

**2 人の会話問題 ①**

　Part 3 では、リスニングの音声が流れる前に設問を読んでおくことが得点アップの手助けになります。設問中の疑問詞と、主語がわかれば、音声の聞くべきポイントがわかります。例えば、「女性」が電話をした「理由」を絞って聞く、などとあらかじめ推測ができるでしょう。

---

Questions 7-9                                               🔊 14

7.　Why did the woman call the man?

　　(A) To inquire about a phone-number

　　(B) To report a problem

　　(C) To ask about his health

　　(D) To deliver some merchandise

8.　Where did the man receive the call?

　　(A) Away from home

　　(B) At a maintenance center

　　(C) At the headquarters' building

　　(D) At a taxi stand

9.　What will the man probably do next?

　　(A) Go back home

　　(B) Check the abnormality

　　(C) Contact the client

　　(D) Report a power failure

## Part 4　Talks

**Strategy for Part 4** ［説明文問題の解き方］

**各種トークの「展開」はほぼ決まっている！②**

　Part 4 によく登場するトークの種類に、「**会議の抜粋（excerpt from a meeting）**」があります。では、会社などで行われる会議において、内容が比較的易しく、部外者（TOEIC 受験者）が聞いても理解できそうな部分とは…おそらく、一般的な連絡事項などの多い、**会議の「始まり」と「終わり」**ではないでしょうか。そこで、まずは会議において、本題に入る前や会議が終わる直前にありがちな台詞やトークの展開に慣れていきましょう。

Questions 10-12

🔊 15

[Office Extension Numbers]

| Name | Extension |
|---|---|
| Joe Benson | 402 |
| Chris McLaren | 410 |
| Terry Garcia | 412 |
| Ronald Freeman | 421 |

**10.** What is the speaker mainly talking about?

　(A) A computer system

　(B) A software company

　(C) A shipping problem

　(D) A cooperate instructor

**11.** What does the speaker recommend?

　(A) Downloading some software

　(B) Attending workshops

　(C) Scheduling online meetings

　(D) Contacting a supervisor

**12.** Look at the graphic. Who is the speaker?

　(A) Joe Benson

　(B) Chris McLaren

　(C) Terry Garcia

　(D) Ronald Freeman

**Part 5** **Incomplete Sentences**

---

**Strategy for Part 5 ［短文穴埋め問題の解き方］**

**品詞識別問題 ① 「文の要素」を思い出そう**

　選択肢がすべて似ていて、同じ語幹の派生語が並んでいる場合、「品詞識別問題」です。選択肢の品詞の種類をチェックして、空所の役割を考えましょう。

空所の役割を考えるためには「文の要素」を整理してみましょう。

| | | |
|---|---|---|
| **S 〈主語〉** Subject | 動作主を表す。人や物事で、「…は、…が」と訳す。 |
| **V 〈動詞〉** Verb | 動作や状態（…する、…である）を表します。 |
| **O 〈目的語〉** Object | 動詞が働きかける対象。（…を、…に）を表す部分です。 |
| **C 〈補語〉** Complement | 主語（S）や目的語（O）を説明する部分。 |

- 目的語になるのは名詞、代名詞、名詞相当語句。補語になるのは名詞、形容詞などです。
- 空所が「名詞」を修飾する場合→「形容詞」または「名詞」が入ります。
- 空所が「動詞」「形容詞」「副詞」を修飾する場合→「副詞」が入ります。

---

13. The seniority system at our company can sometimes seem ------- to someone who is new to the job.

    (A) confusing　　(B) confusion　　(C) confuse　　(D) confusingly

14. Topics at the technical support team's meeting ------- customer management.

    (A) include　　(B) includes　　(C) including　　(D) inclusion

15. After launching their new camera model, the company received ------- that the automated timer was not working properly.

    (A) complainer　　(B) complaints　　(C) complains　　(D) complained

16. This month's TV commercial will surely ------- sales in the metropolitan area.

    (A) stimulate　　(B) stimulation　　(C) to stimulate　　(D) stimulated

## Part 6  Text Completion

**Strategy for Part 6** ［長文穴埋め問題の解き方］

**文書の種類 ①**

　Part 6 に登場する**文書の単語数は大体 100 語前後**ですので、それほど長くはありません。しかもその種類は非常に限られています。その中の 1 つが「**社内回覧（memo）**」です。学生にはあまり馴染みがないかもしれませんが、これはどのような時に出されるものか、考えてみましょう。多くは「多数の社員に、何かを知らせたい」時ですね。もし少数の社員宛てに個別に連絡するならば、通常は e-mail などを使うのではないでしょうか。

Questions 17-20 refer to the following memo.

---

To: All employees at White Hills Software
From: Fred Choi, General Affairs Section
Subject: Free online seminar series
Date: July 21


We would like to let you know that our company will offer all employees a series of free online business English classes next month. ------- international communication
　　　　　　　　　　　　　　　　　　　　　　　　　　**17.**
skills are needed in our industry, your attendance is highly recommended. Since all the classes will be held online, you can attend them anywhere the Internet is available. The instructors are experienced and familiar with our industry, we are sure that their classes will be ------- and helpful to your everyday work with foreign companies.
　　　　　　　　　　　**18.**
-------. Thus, your computer has to be equipped with a camera and a microphone.
**19.**
The timetable ------- on the company Web site today. For further information, please
　　　　　　　**20.**
contact us at extension 210 or e-mail us at general@whitehills.com.

---

**17.** (A) Regardless of　(B) Even though　(C) Considering that　(D) Along with

**18.** (A) information　　　(B) informative　　(C) informed　　　(D) inform

**19.** (A) We have sufficient numbers of computers for you all.
　　　(B) We understand that you are too busy to come to the classroom.
　　　(C) You will be allocated to your classes next week.
　　　(D) You will have interactive communication practice in class.

**20.** (A) will be posted　(B) will post　　　(C) will be posting　(D) will have posted

設問パターン ①

Unit 2 で紹介した Part 7 の設問の種類のうち、**1. 文書の目的・概要を問うタイプ**について説明します。

2016 年の「新形式」への変更以来、TOEIC L&R のリーディングは「受験者に文書『全体』を読ませる」ための出題傾向が強くなりました。皆さんは Part 7 を解く際、文書のあちらこちらをかいつまんで読み、文書と設問の間を頻繁に行ったり来たりしていませんか。この解き方で時間を無駄にすることも多いのです。「まずは一通り、文書をすべて読む」…少なくとも練習の際は、これを心がけてみてはいかがでしょうか。全体を読めば文書の目的や概要はたいていわかります。さらに、どこに何が書いてあるかを把握できていれば、「行ったり来たり」も減り、より多くの問題が解けるようになるでしょう。

Questions 21-25 refer to the following advertisement.

### *'Why don't you sell your used PC?'*

Don't you have an old PC in storage that you don't use anymore? Eco-Friends PC, Ltd. can help you sell it at the highest price in your local area. It does not matter if your PC is working fine or not working at all. Even if your PC is too hard to repair, any of its parts could be reused in another computer.

Please see the instructions below:

*1. Complete the form*

First, you will need to complete an application form, which can be downloaded from our Web site.

*2. Send your PC to us*

Please send us your PC as a fragile item along with the correct form to the address listed below by certified mail. We will cover the shipping costs.

*3. Consider our estimated price*

Once we've received your PC and carefully examined it, we will immediately call you with the details of its condition and our estimated price. Please let us know if you accept it or not within two business days after you have received our call. If you are happy with our price, we will deposit the money in your bank account on the same day as your notice of acceptance.

*4. If you do not accept our estimated price*

If you are not satisfied with our estimated price, we will send your PC back to you. Please note, you will be charged 15 pounds for the return shipping costs in this case.

**Eco-Friends PC, Ltd.  11 Parkside Lane, Longsight, West Ham  W10 5AP**

~ We are an official eco-friendly company certified by West Ham City. ~

21. Who is the instruction paper most likely intended for?

    (A) Internet providers

    (B) Computer users

    (C) Appliance stores

    (D) Parts suppliers

22. What is available on the Web site?

    (A) An estimated cost

    (B) An application form

    (C) A list of parts

    (D) A discount coupon

23. What does Eco-Friends PC, Ltd. do for its customers?

    (A) Contacts the manufacturer

    (B) Delivers components

    (C) Evaluates their hardware

    (D) Collects their computers

24. The word "certified" in paragraph 3, line 2, is closest in meaning to

    (A) enclosed

    (B) criticized

    (C) identified

    (D) registered

25. What is suggested about the service?

    (A) Items beyond repair can still be sold.

    (B) Any documents need to be submitted online.

    (C) The company always covers shipment costs.

    (D) Customers have to pay a deposit.

## Vocabulary Check!

Choose an appropriate translation for the following words.

🔊 16

| | | |
|---|---|---|
| **1.** celebrate (   ) | **2.** accommodation (   ) | **3.** decade (   ) |
| **4.** ban (   ) | **5.** notify (   ) | **6.** policy (   ) |
| **7.** suggestion (   ) | **8.** survey (   ) | **9.** advertise (   ) |
| **10.** improve (   ) | **11.** introduce (   ) | **12.** regulation (   ) |

| | | | |
|---|---|---|---|
| a. 導入する | b. 祝う | c. 規定 | d. 10 年間 |
| e. 改良する | f. 禁止する | g. 知らせる | h. 宿泊 |
| i. 調査 | j. 宣伝する | k. 方針 | l. 提案 |

## 🎧 Listening Section

### Part 1　Photographs

**Strategy for Part 1　［写真描写問題の解き方］**

**風景、室内の写真 ①**

　風景、室内の写真では、There is ～, There are ～（～があります）で始まり、前の名詞を具体的にするための位置関係を表す表現で終わる選択肢が出現します。写真の「何が」「どこに」あるか、に注目して聞きましょう。

**1.**

Ⓐ Ⓑ Ⓒ Ⓓ

**2.**　🔊 17

Ⓐ Ⓑ Ⓒ Ⓓ

### Part 2　Question-Response

**Strategy for Part 2　［応答問題の解き方］**

**疑問詞で始まる疑問文 ④　What，Whose，Why**

　Part 2 では、疑問詞で始まる設問に対して "Yes" や "No" で始まる選択肢はほぼ不正解です。Why で始まる疑問文は基本的には「理由」を聞いていますが、Why に対して単純に Because で始まる選択肢も誤答を誘っている場合が多いので気をつけましょう。

🔊 18

**3.**　Mark your answer on your answer sheet.　　　Ⓐ Ⓑ Ⓒ

**4.**　Mark your answer on your answer sheet.　　　Ⓐ Ⓑ Ⓒ

**5.**　Mark your answer on your answer sheet.　　　Ⓐ Ⓑ Ⓒ

**6.**　Mark your answer on your answer sheet.　　　Ⓐ Ⓑ Ⓒ

## Part 3 Conversations

Questions 7-9                                              🔊 19

7.  Who is the man shopping for?
    (A) His manager
    (B) His wife
    (C) His daughter
    (D) His room-mate

8.  What time does the florist usually close?
    (A) At 6 P.M.
    (B) At 7 P.M.
    (C) At 8 P.M.
    (D) At 9 P.M.

9.  What did the man probably do in the morning?
    (A) Baked cookies
    (B) Reserved a ticket
    (C) Dried his laundry
    (D) Bought a cake

## Part 4  Talks

**Strategy for Part 4** ［説明文問題の解き方］

**各種トークの「展開」はほぼ決まっている！③**

　Part 4 でよく登場するトークに「**宣伝広告（advertisement, radio advertisement）**」があります。宣伝されるのは主に、①商品、②事業所（店、レストランなど）です。聞き手を惹きつけるために、疑問文で始まることも多く、続いて、宣伝したいもののメリットを列挙していきます。そして、「これは何の広告でしょうか？」など『概要・基本情報』を問う問題、「割引」「特典」「期間」などの『詳細情報』を問う問題がよく見られます。

Questions 10-12　　　　　　　　　　　　　　　　　　🔊 20

10. What most likely happened to Best Eastern before July 1?

    (A) It held a series of events.

    (B) It opened another branch.

    (C) It was relocated.

    (D) It was refurbished.

11. What is the business offering until July 21?

    (A) Free access to its private beach

    (B) Reduced accommodation fees

    (C) A promotional code

    (D) A series of events

12. What are the listeners advised to do to join the events?

    (A) Purchase a ticket beforehand

    (B) Reserve a room online

    (C) Visit the reception

    (D) Present their ID card

## Part 5  Incomplete Sentences

### Strategy for Part 5 ［短文穴埋め問題の解き方］

品詞識別問題 ②  「基本5文型」と「第2文型」、「第3文型」の見分け方

文の要素を使って、基本5文型をまとめると次のようになります。

第1文型（S+V）　　　　例：He smiles.「彼は微笑む。」

第2文型（S+V+C）　　　例：I am tall.「私は背が高い。」

第3文型（S+V+O）　　　例：She loves her mother.「彼女は母親を愛しています。」

第4文型（S+V+O+O）　　例：He gave me some advice.「彼からアドバイスをされました。」

第5文型（S+V+O+C）　　例：She keeps it secret.「彼女はそのことを秘密にしています。」

### 「第2文型」と「第3文型」の見分け方

この5つの文型の中で、重要で、混同しやすいのが「第2文型」と「第3文型」です。

第2文型（S+V+C）

SとCはイコールの関係です。

Richard　is　　tall.　　「リチャードは背が高いです。」
　<S>　　<V> <C: 形容詞 >　Richard＝tall

第3文型（S+V+O）

Oは「…を」「…に」の部分です。SとOはイコールの関係ではありません。

Richard　loves　her.　　「リチャードは彼女を愛しています。」
　<S>　　<V>　　<O>　　Richard ≠ her （リチャードは彼女とイコールではありません）

---

**13.** I had my work ------- by four o'clock this morning.

    (A) does        (B) did        (C) doing        (D) done

**14.** It is important to make ------- use of serving robots at our local branches.

    (A) efficient       (B) efficiency       (C) efficiently       (D) efficiencies

**15.** Congestion at the time of check-out has become much more ------- now that the new computer system is operating.

    (A) managing       (B) manage       (C) manageable       (D) management

**16.** Patricia Anderson, who ------- the musical theater will donate proceeds from the concerts to a local children's charity.

    (A) founded       (B) foundation       (C) founding       (D) found

## Part 6  Text Completion

Questions 17-20 refer to the following letter.

---

Southwest Coast Hotel
241 Anson Street, Tamuning
Guam, 96931

February 19

Dear Valued Guests,

You may have heard that the city ------- a total smoking ban in public buildings,
**17.**
including hotels. Following the new regulation, which takes ------- on March 1, we
**18.**
would like to inform you that we have also renewed our smoking policy. -------, the
**19.**
separate smoking room on the first floor is no longer available.

-------. We have already set up an outside smoking space behind the building for all
**20.**
of our smoking guests to use during their stay.

We would appreciate your understanding of our new smoking policy and look
forward to your future stay with us.

Julia Jonathan
General Manager, Southwest Coast Hotel

---

**17.** (A) will introduce　　(B) is introduced　　(C) introduced　　(D) has been introduced

**18.** (A) effective　　(B) effectively　　(C) effect　　(D) effectiveness

**19.** (A) For example　　(B) Alternatively　　(C) Even so　　(D) Similarly

**20.** (A) However, hotels are exempted from these new rules.

　　 (B) Accordingly, we decided to move the room upstairs.

　　 (C) The new regulation will not be applied to all of the hotels in the city.

　　 (D) This does not mean a complete smoking ban for the whole premises.

**設問パターン ②**

　Unit 2 で紹介した **3. 選択肢を文書と照らし合わせるタイプ**ですが、一般に「解答するのに最も時間が かかる設問」と考えられます。なぜでしょうか。

　まず設問の形はほかと見分けがつきやすく、What is suggested / implied / indicated / mentioned / stated / true about ～？と決まっています。では、「～について、何が述べられていますか？」という設 問の答えを選ぶ際、私たちは何をしなければならないでしょうか…そう、**4 つの選択肢を 1 つずつ文書 と照らし合わせ、確認する必要があるの**です。しかも、文中の表現がそのまま選択肢になっていること は極めてまれで、ほとんどが別の表現に言い換えられています。

　最初のうちは、本番でこのような問題に時間を使いすぎないよう、くれぐれも注意してください。しか し、このタイプは Part 7 の 54 問中 15 問前後を占めますので、皆さんがより高いスコアを目指すように なった時は、正解数を増やしたい問題とも言えます。

Questions 21-25 refer to the following e-mail.

| To: | Patrick Lowney <p.lowney@mina-accounting.com> |
|---|---|
| From: | Ellie Fisher <e.fisher@grandhotel.co.ch> |
| Date: | December 2 |
| Subject: | Winter events in 2023 |

Dear Mr. Lowney,

Thank you for your continued patronage. For our 20th anniversary, we are planning to offer our valued guests a series of special events during the new year holidays. We would appreciate it if you could spare a few minutes to answer our online customer survey about the events.

Referring to our guests' answers, we will finalize the details of the event content and schedules. If you join the survey, you may be invited to one of the events. Our tentative plans are as follows:

December 31: New Year's Eve Jazz Concert
We are inviting up to 50 people to a music concert at the banquet hall. The renowned band, Sothern Cross Avenue, will take you to the wonderland of jazz music. Children aged under 5 are not allowed to enter. Let us celebrate a wonderful 2023 with lovely music! — [1] —.

January 3: Let's Enjoy Snowboarding!
Just before the grand-opening of our third private slope, it will be opened to novice snowboarders. Experienced instructors will give you a lot of tips to improve your skills. Why don't you enjoy early access to the brand-new slope? — [2] —.

January 6: New Year's Dinner

On the final day of our event week, Theresa Austin, our chief chef, will be serving up to 70 of the guests a special dinner. To celebrate her winning the international culinary contest 2022, some of the dishes will be cooked based upon the recipes she created for the contest. — [3] —.

If you are interested in any of the above, please click the link grandhotel.ch/survey/23, answer the questionnaire and apply for one of the events. We are anticipating a lot of applicants, so there will likely be a ballot for the invitations. Winners will be notified by e-mail by December 20 at the latest. — [4] —.

We look forward to hearing your evaluations, suggestions or opinions.

Sincerely,
Ellie Fisher
Promotion Manager, Grand Hotel Geneva

**21.** What is the purpose of the e-mail?
(A) To ask for suggestions
(B) To invite guests to the events
(C) To advertise the grand opening
(D) To answer a customer survey

**22.** What is true about the hotel?
(A) It holds some events every winter.
(B) It will be remodelled in December.
(C) It has been highly evaluated for years.
(D) It was opened a few decades ago.

**23.** What is suggested about Patrick Lowney?
(A) He will be attending an event.
(B) He will be taking a vacation.
(C) He has conducted a survey online.
(D) He has stayed at the hotel before.

**24.** The word "anticipating" in paragraph 6, line 2, is closest in meaning to
(A) addressing
(B) succeeding
(C) expecting
(D) certifying

**25.** In which of the positions marked [1], [2], [3], and [4] does the following sentence best belong?
"Considering its size, the number of participants is limited to 30."
(A) [1]
(B) [2]
(C) [3]
(D) [4]

## Vocabulary Check!

Choose an appropriate translation for the following words.

🔊 21

1. apologize (　　)　　2. browse (　　)　　3. furniture (　　)

4. rigid (　　)　　5. discount (　　)　　6. exchange (　　)

7. unfortunately (　　)　　8. remodel (　　)　　9. manual (　　)

10. inconvenience (　　)　　11. affordable (　　)　　12. eligible (　　)

---

a. 家具　　　　b. 交換する　　　c. 固い　　　　d. 値引き

e. 改良する、新たにする　　　　f. 手に入れられる、手ごろな

g. 不便　　　h. マニュアル　　i. 残念なことに　　j. 謝る、謝罪する

k. 能力のある　　l. 見て回る

# 🎧 Listening Section

## Part 1   Photographs

### Strategy for Part 1 ［写真描写問題の解き方］

**風景、室内の写真 ②**

　風景、室内の写真では「～されたところです」を表す、現在完了形の受動態「has / have+been+ 過去分詞」を含む選択肢が出現します。動作が完了した状態を表しているので、写真で表すことが十分可能です。正解である可能性も高いので注意して聞きましょう。

**1.**

Ⓐ Ⓑ Ⓒ Ⓓ

**2.**　　　🔊 22

Ⓐ Ⓑ Ⓒ Ⓓ

## Part 2   Question-Response

### Strategy for Part 2 ［応答問題の解き方］

**一般疑問文 ①　Do you ~ ?,  Does he ~ ?**

　一般疑問文に対する答え方は、例えば中学校の英語の授業では Do you have a pen? に対して Yes, I do. や No, I don't. が基本的な答え方だと習いました。しかし、Part 2 においてはそのような基本的な答え方は誤答選択肢として頻出します。引っかからないように注意しましょう。

🔊 23

**3.**　Mark your answer on your answer sheet.　　Ⓐ Ⓑ Ⓒ

**4.**　Mark your answer on your answer sheet.　　Ⓐ Ⓑ Ⓒ

**5.**　Mark your answer on your answer sheet.　　Ⓐ Ⓑ Ⓒ

**6.**　Mark your answer on your answer sheet.　　Ⓐ Ⓑ Ⓒ

Questions 7-9　　　　　　　　　　　　　　　　　　　🔊 24

**7.** What are the speakers discussing?

　(A) Climbing sticks

　(B) A tablet computer

　(C) A suitcase

　(D) Sports shoes

**8.** What does the man ask about?

　(A) The shoes comfort

　(B) The total cost of the gadget

　(C) The warranty options

　(D) The steepness of the slopes

**9.** What will Daisy probably do next?

　(A) Look for a wider size

　(B) Look for a steep mountain

　(C) Try on the basic model

　(D) Try on the high-end model

## Part 4  Talks

### Strategy for Part 4 ［説明文問題の解き方］

**「図表問題」の解き方 ①**

　2016 年 5 月の公開テストから「新形式」に変わった TOEIC L&R、Part 3 と Part 4 では **「図表問題（グラフや図などを見ながら解く問題）」** が新登場しました。

　設問が必ず "Look at the graphic." で始まるこの図表問題、テストでは Part 3 と Part 4 に、合計 5 問出題されます（例：Part 3 に 3 問、Part 4 に 2 問）。

　この種類の問題を解く前に、①選択肢と図表をチェック、②**「選択肢に並んでいる語句は、トークからは聞こえてこない」** と考えましょう（聞こえたら図表が不要になってしまいます）。

Questions 10-12                                    🔊 25

### ~ The Special Events at Jenner's Mason ~

| Venue | Event |
|---|---|
| 1st Floor | "Rich Tastes from the South" |
| 2nd Floor | "Furniture for Your House" |
| 3rd Floor | "Autumn Fashion Week" |
| 4th Floor | "European Antique Fair" |

**10.** What is the announcement mainly about?

(A) A grand opening

(B) A renovation plan

(C) Some new products

(D) Some seasonal sales

**11.** Look at the graphic. Which floor will most likely be renovated?

(A) 1st Floor

(B) 2nd Floor

(C) 3rd Floor

(D) 4th Floor

**12.** What can the listeners do online?

(A) Apply for membership

(B) Get a discount coupon

(C) Browse for items

(D) Send a gift card

## Part 5　Incomplete Sentences

### Strategy for Part 5 ［短文穴埋め問題の解き方］

**文法問題 ①　接続詞の基本ルール**

　S+V のかたまりを含む文を「節」と言います。英語の文章ではこの「節」が 1 文（大文字で始まってピリオドで終わるまで）で 2 つ以上あったら接続詞でつながなければいけません。

☆「等位接続詞」と「従属接続詞」

接続詞には大きく分けて「等位接続詞」と「従属接続詞（従位接続詞ともいう）」があります。

「等位接続詞」は「節」と「節」、「句」と「句」、「語」と「語」を対等に結びつけます。(for, and, nor, but, or, yet, so など)

> Kate can speak English **and** French.
>        ↑対等（語と語）
> 「ケイトは英語とフランス語を話すことができます。」

「従属接続詞」は「節」と「節」を結びますが、接続詞のある節が、従属節（時、理由、条件を表す）、ない節が主節、というように「差」をつけて結びます。
(時を表す when, while, as, after, before, since、原因目的を表す because, as, so that, now that、条件、譲歩のかたまりを作る if, unless, in case, although, though などがあります)

> I like Suzan **because** she is kind.
> 〈主節〉　　なぜなら　〈従属節〉理由を表しています。
> 「私はスーザンが好きです、なぜなら彼女は優しいからです。」

**13.** My father went home ------- I watched a movie.

(A) and　　　　(B) no　　　　(C) yet　　　　(D) or

**14.** It was not long ------- Jim took the post of store manager.

(A) list　　　　(B) before　　　　(C) chance　　　　(D) time

**15.** ------- the company increases the number of workers to 15, most customers will be satisfied.

(A) But　　　　(B) So　　　　(C) And　　　　(D) If

**16.** Cell-phones should be turned off ------- the courses are served in this classy restaurant.

(A) while　　　　(B) meantime　　　　(C) that　　　　(D) therefore

## Part 6  Text Completion

Questions 17-20 refer to the following e-mail.

---

To: Customer Service <customer@worldpc.com>
From: Sean Perlman <s.perlman@coachstage.net>
Date: March 30
Subject: Missing items

I purchased a touch-screen tablet, TPC21A, from your online store last week and the item reached me as scheduled. -------, the stylus pen for it was not enclosed in the
**17.**
package. -------. However, it was advertised that, during the sale, the complimentary
**18.**
stylus pen would be offered with the tablet. Since I need to use it for my presentation next Friday, I would appreciate it if you could ------- the stylus immediately.
**19.**

------- the above, I am quite satisfied with the item, which runs faster and more
**20.**
smoothly than I expected. Moreover, I am impressed by the affordable prices you offer and I look forward to buying other home appliances from this shop in the future.

Thank you in advance.
Sean

---

**17.** (A) Furthermore　(B) Eventually　(C) Specifically　(D) Regrettably

**18.** (A) I understand that the stylus is normally sold separately.
(B) I thought I was eligible to get a full refund.
(C) I was supposed to receive a replacement from you.
(D) I was so disappointed that it was out of stock then.

**19.** (A) remit　(B) present　(C) proceed　(D) dispatch

**20.** (A) Apart from　(B) Because of　(C) According to　(D) Just like

Questions 21-25 refer to the following e-mails.

| To: | Customer Care Team <customercare@bicappliance.co.uk> |
|---|---|
| From: | Ronald Brooks <ronaldbrooks@finglands.com> |
| Date: | 20 September |
| Subject: | My request |

I purchased a vacuum cleaner at my local BIC Appliance shop on the 15th of September. Unfortunately, I found a tear on its hose and the cleaner was not working properly. To have the part exchanged for a new one, I filled out the replacement request form attached to the item and sent both the part and the form to the address shown in the instructions the following day.

Although I followed the exchange policy on your Web site correctly and completed the request process within the required time limit, as of today, I have not received a replacement from you. Since I am expecting guests soon, I need this vacuum cleaner as quickly as possible. Could you please check the status of my request and update me as soon as possible?

Thank you.
Ronald

| To: | Ronald Brooks <ronaldbrooks@finglands.com> |
|---|---|
| From: | Megan Little <meganlittle@bicappliance.co.uk> |
| Date: | 21 September |
| Subject: | Re: My request |

Dear Mr. Brooks,

Thank you very much for your shopping at BIC Appliance. I am writing in response to your e-mail that we received yesterday regarding your request. We immediately checked it out on our online database and examined the purchase records from the Stirling branch. Consequently, it turned out that your request is pending and the part you sent us is temporarily stored at our warehouse in Chesterfield.

This does not mean you made any mistakes in the exchange process. Although there have been some recent changes in our exchange policy, regrettably we had not updated our Web site when you completed the request process. From the 1st of September, all customers are required to return not only the part but the whole item for us to examine the entire product more thoroughly.

We apologize for any inconvenience this mistake has caused you and were wondering if you could send us the rest of the appliance back, too. We will cover your additional shipping fee. Also, as a token of our apology, I am sending you a 50 percent discount coupon for a future purchase at any of our shops.

Kind regards,
Megan Little
Customer Care Team Representative, BIC Appliance Co., Ltd.

**21.** According to the first e-mail, what is the problem?
(A) A shipment has not arrived yet.
(B) An item is malfunctioning.
(C) A manual is not enclosed.
(D) A part does not fit the product.

**22.** What did Ronald Brooks NOT do on and after 15 September?
(A) Completed a form
(B) Shipped an item
(C) Placed another order
(D) Checked the instructions

**23.** According to the second e-mail, what will Ronald Brooks receive?
(A) A voucher   (B) A part   (C) A replacement   (D) An invoice

**24.** The word "examined" in paragraph 1, line 3, in the second e-mail, is closest in meaning to
(A) preserved   (B) passed   (C) collected   (D) inspected

**25.** What is implied about Ronald Brooks?
(A) He followed the previous exchange policy.
(B) He missed updating his contact details online.
(C) He has recently moved to Stirling.
(D) He lives near the Chesterfield warehouse.

# UNIT 6
# Transportation

## Vocabulary Check!

Choose an appropriate translation for the following words.

🔊 26

| | | |
|---|---|---|
| **1.** proceed ( ) | **2.** detour ( ) | **3.** eventually ( ) |
| **4.** repair ( ) | **5.** fare ( ) | **6.** feature ( ) |
| **7.** monorail ( ) | **8.** pave ( ) | **9.** destination ( ) |
| **10.** congestion ( ) | **11.** completely ( ) | **12.** venue ( ) |

| | | | |
|---|---|---|---|
| a. ついに、結局は | b. 特徴 | c. 迂回する | d. 開催地 |
| e. 料金 | f. 補修する | g. 完全に | h. 混雑 |
| i. すすむ | j. 目的地 | k. 舗装する | l. モノレール |

# 🎧 Listening Section

## Part 1 Photographs

### Strategy for Part 1 ［写真描写問題の解き方］

**複数人物の写真 ③**

　写真描写問題で、主語を表す表現は audience「観客」、pedestrian「歩行者」、passenger「乗客」、driver「運転手」、shopkeeper「店員」、vendor「販売員」などがあります。
種類はそれほど多くないので覚えておきましょう。

**1.**

Ⓐ Ⓑ Ⓒ Ⓓ

**2.** 🔊 27

Ⓐ Ⓑ Ⓒ Ⓓ

## Part 2 Question-Response

### Strategy for Part 2 ［応答問題の解き方］

**一般疑問文 ②　Are you ~ ?, Is he ~ ?**

　Be 動詞で始まる一般疑問文においても、典型的な答え方、例えば Are you a student? に対して Yes, I am. や No, I'm not. が出てきたら誤答である可能性が高いです。

🔊 28

**3.** Mark your answer on your answer sheet.　　Ⓐ Ⓑ Ⓒ

**4.** Mark your answer on your answer sheet.　　Ⓐ Ⓑ Ⓒ

**5.** Mark your answer on your answer sheet.　　Ⓐ Ⓑ Ⓒ

**6.** Mark your answer on your answer sheet.　　Ⓐ Ⓑ Ⓒ

**Strategy for Part 3** ［会話問題の解き方］

**図表を含む問題 ①**

　図表を含む問題では、音声が流れる前に設問と図表を見ておく必要があります。しかし図表を見ただけで正解できてしまってはリスニングの問題となりません。問題の少なくとも１つは、音声と図表の内容の両方から正解を導き出すようにつくられています。

Questions 7-9　　　　　　　　　　　　　　　　　　　　　🔊 29

## Central Hills Station

| Train Number | Departure Station | Status | Estimated time of arrival |
|---|---|---|---|
| WC 012 | The West End | Arrived | 13:00 |
| SC 055 | Sixth Avenue | On time | 14:00 |
| GC 334 | Green Garden | On time | 14:30 |
| LC 906 | The lake district | Delayed | 15:30 |

7. Look at the graphic. Which station is Jonathan Spacy traveling from?
   (A) The West End
   (B) Sixth Avenue
   (C) Green Garden
   (D) The Lake District

8. According to the man, what is the cause of the trouble?
   (A) A storm
   (B) An accident
   (C) A hurricane
   (D) An electrical failure

9. What does the man suggest to do at Central Hills Station?
   (A) To see the weather forecast
   (B) To check a Web site
   (C) To wait for the trouble to subside
   (D) To eat something

## Part 4　Talks

**Strategy for Part 4** ［説明文問題の解き方］

「図表問題」の解き方 ②

　「図表問題（グラフや図などを見て解く問題）」で出題される図表の中に、「フロア・マップ」や「ルート・マップ」のような**「地図系」**のものがあります。このような図表は、どこに注意すべきでしょう。

　例えば、(A) Room 1, (B) Room 2, ... のように選択肢が並んでいる場合、トークの中で「Room 1」とはまず言いません。それでは図表が不要になってしまいますよね。しかし、図をよく見ると、「Supply Room（備品室）」のように「目印になる場所」などが載っていませんか。この**「目印になる場所」に注意**して、トークを聴いてみてください。

Questions 10-12　🔊 30

Town Map

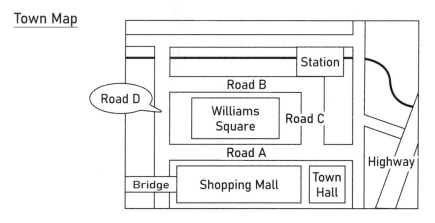

10. What is the broadcast mainly about?

    (A) The event schedule

    (B) The location of the venue

    (C) Highway repairs

    (D) Traffic updates

11. Look at the graphic. Which most likely is Dales Road?

    (A) Road A

    (B) Road B

    (C) Road C

    (D) Road D

12. What does the town suggest the listeners do after 3 P.M.?

    (A) Show their parking permit

    (B) Walk to the venue

    (C) Use public transportation

    (D) Follow the bus route

## Part 5　Incomplete Sentences

### Strategy for Part 5 ［短文穴埋め問題の解き方］

**文法問題②　接続詞 vs 前置詞のパターン**

選択肢に前置詞、接続副詞、接続詞が並ぶ、「接続詞」vs「前置詞」の問題は Part 5 で頻出します。

**☆接続詞と前置詞の見分け方**

接続詞：後ろには S+V のかたまりである「節」がきます。

前置詞：前置詞の後に続くのは必ず「名詞」もしくは「名詞相当語句」です。

接続詞 vs 前置詞の典型例（Part 5 でよく出題される識別）

| 接続詞 | 前置詞句 |
|---|---|
| because | because of<br>「〜なので」 |
| while | during<br>「〜のあいだ」 |
| since | due to<br>「〜の理由で」 |
| although | despite<br>「〜にもかかわらず」 |
| unless | without<br>「〜がなければ」 |

空所の後が、名詞句なのか、節なのかを見て、空所に入れる語や品詞を選びましょう。

---

**13.** ------- I was staying in Oxford, I visited the local church to see my friends.

    (A) However     (B) Being     (C) During     (D) While

**14.** ------- a constantly weak economy, there has been an increase in sales in the fast-food industry.

    (A) Despite     (B) Instead     (C) Although     (D) Because

**15.** I'll lend you some money ------- you promise me to pay it back in a month.

    (A) as good as     (B) as long as     (C) as well as     (D) as rich as

**16.** Your member card cannot be processed ------- your picture has been submitted.

    (A) until     (B) once     (C) between     (D) besides

# Part 6  Text Completion

## Strategy for Part 6 ［長文穴埋め問題の解き方］

**設問タイプ ①**

Part 6の設問は、「**1. 文脈に関係なく解ける設問**」と「**2. 文脈に沿って解く設問**」の2つに大別できます。「**1. 文脈に関係なく解ける**」とは、言い換えれば、空所を含む1つの文だけを読めば解けるということ、つまりPart 5の設問と同じです。具体的には、「品詞を選ぶ問題」「前置詞を選ぶ問題」「関係代名詞を選ぶ問題」などが挙げられます。このような設問は4問（1文書）中1問程度と少数ですが、時間をかけずに解答できます。もしテストで残り時間が少なく、文書をすべて読むことができない場合でも、Part 5の設問と同じ感覚で確実に解いておくことをお勧めします。

Questions 17-20 refer to the following notice.

---

Bus Services to be Suspended on Some Routes

To all passengers:

Due to road repair works on Acton Street and Manchester Avenue, Coastridge Bus Company ------- operating its bus services on routes 3, 7, 15, 24 and 41 from 10:00 A.M.
**17.**
to 8:00 P.M. tomorrow. -------. This will highly likely cause heavy traffic on other roads,
**18.**
especially around the Archway Park Area.

　For passengers going to the airport tomorrow, we recommend taking our temporary bus services from the East Terminal, ------- will make detours to avoid the busy
**19.**
area. -------, they are advised to take the subway to Vermont Station near the airport
**20.**
tomorrow.

We apologize for any inconvenience this may cause you.

---

**17.** (A) will suspend

(B) will be suspended

(C) will have been suspending

(D) will have suspended

**18.** (A) These roads will be completely closed for several hours.

(B) The road construction project is likely to be revised soon.

(C) The new timetable has been posted on our Web site.

(D) A new bus terminal will be opened next month.

**19.** (A) that　　　(B) it　　　(C) whose　　　(D) where

**20.** (A) Eventually　　(B) Alternatively　　(C) For details　　(D) If possible

**Strategy for Part 7 ［読解問題の解き方］**

**ダブル・パッセージ型**

設問176から設問185までは、2つの文書を読んで5問の設問に答える「ダブル・パッセージ型」が2セット続きます。読む文書が2つあり、かつリーディングセクションの終わり近くに出てくるので、漠然と「難しい」というイメージを持つ人が多いようです。

しかし、この「ダブル・パッセージ型」、両文書からヒントを見つけないと解けない設問は、実際5問（1セット）中、1、2問しか出ません。つまりそのほかの設問は、どちらか一方の文書でヒントを見つければ解けるということです。

「シングル・パッセージ型（文書1つ）」と同様に、全体の「ストーリー」をつかむため、まずは2つの文書を一気に読み通しましょう。その上で、設問にある "According to the Web site …" などの、どちらの文書にヒントがあるのかを示す語句に注意し、効率よくヒントを見つける練習をしてみてはいかがでしょうか。

Questions 21-25 refer to the following Web page and e-mail.

---

### The New Ticket Purchasing App 'Fast Seater' is Now Available!

For greater convenience, Northern Trains introduced a new ticket purchasing application "Fast Seater" on October 1. It allows customers to purchase tickets far more easily on their smartphones and they will no longer need paper tickets for their journeys. Please see the following instructions and features of our new app:

#### 1. Download the app
Please install "Fast Seater" from this Web site on your smartphone. Payments can be made by credit card, using our previous online system. You can now connect payment apps such as "Easy Pay" or "Quick Pay" to our app for more convenience.

#### 2. Seating Charts
After you input your destination and the number of tickets required, please tap the "seating map" button. With the new app, customers can book their seats exactly where they prefer to sit. By tapping the button, the seating chart of the train will appear on the screen. Then, please choose the seats you prefer. Customers can make seat reservations 30 minutes before their departure.
Please note that payment must be made within 10 minutes of your booking.

#### 3. Paperless Boarding
On the trains, you do not need to have any paper tickets with you at all. For ticket inspection, please just show the train conductor your online ticket on the screen of your smartphone.

*We look forward to traveling with you soon.*
Customer Support, Northern Trains Co., Ltd.

---

Dear Customer Support,

Hi, I booked three seats on the train to Frinton for November 20 using 'Fast Seater' on my smartphone and tried to pay for them. However, my smartphone keeps freezing at the payment stage on your app and I cannot proceed further. Incidentally, I have confirmed there is no problem with my smartphone at an appliance store and my credit card works properly on other online payments. How can I sort this problem out?

Regards,
Peter Walsh

**21.** What is the purpose of the Web page?
  (A) To announce the latest system
  (B) To advertise a new appliance
  (C) To promote a special sale
  (D) To report a technical problem

**22.** What are customers advised to do to use the new system?
  (A) Register their bank account details
  (B) Download security software
  (C) Link specific applications together
  (D) Update their personal information

**23.** What is suggested about Peter Walsh?
  (A) He lives near an appliance store.
  (B) He has made some payments by credit card.
  (C) He purchased his device online.
  (D) He often goes on business trips to Frington.

**24.** What will Peter Walsh most likely do on November 20?
  (A) Cancel his tickets                (B) Check his bank account
  (C) Present his smartphone            (D) Change his destination

**25.** What is mentioned about the app?
  (A) It has increased the number of customers.
  (B) It is available on all types of smartphones.
  (C) It provides customers with a chart.
  (D) It shows customers the total fare amount.

UNIT **7**
Travel

## Vocabulary Check!

Choose an appropriate translation for the following words.　🔊 31

| | | |
|---|---|---|
| **1.** preserve ( ) | **2.** tropical ( ) | **3.** description ( ) |
| **4.** technical ( ) | **5.** alternative ( ) | **6.** confectionary ( ) |
| **7.** craftsmanship ( ) | **8.** traditional ( ) | **9.** picturesque ( ) |
| **10.** handrail ( ) | **11.** outstanding ( ) | **12.** moderate ( ) |

| | | | |
|---|---|---|---|
| a. 南国の | b. 代わりの | c. 説明書 | d. お菓子の |
| e. 温暖な | f. 手すり | g. 目立つ | h. 絵のような |
| i. 伝統的な | j. 玄人精神 | k. 技術的な | l. 保存する |

## 🎧 Listening Section

### Part 1　Photographs

**Strategy for Part 1 ［写真描写問題の解き方］**

**人物 1 人の写真 ②**

　人物が 1 人だけ写っている写真、または 1 人の人物にフォーカスを当てていて、主語がすべて同じである場合、主語の後の動詞部分が写真と一致しているかどうかについて集中して聞きましょう。

**1.**

Ⓐ Ⓑ Ⓒ Ⓓ

**2.**  32

Ⓐ Ⓑ Ⓒ Ⓓ

### Part 2　Question-Response

**Strategy for Part 2 ［応答問題の解き方］**

**一般疑問文 ③　Did they ~ ?, Were you ~ ?**

　質問に対して「わかりません」と答えたり、詳細情報についてコメントしたり、質問に対して質問で返していても会話がスムーズに流れていれば正解です。

🔊 33

**3.**　Mark your answer on your answer sheet.　Ⓐ Ⓑ Ⓒ

**4.**　Mark your answer on your answer sheet.　Ⓐ Ⓑ Ⓒ

**5.**　Mark your answer on your answer sheet.　Ⓐ Ⓑ Ⓒ

**6.**　Mark your answer on your answer sheet.　Ⓐ Ⓑ Ⓒ

**図表を含む問題 ②**

　図表を含む問題の図表の種類には、表だけではなく、クーポンや案内、地図や平面図、棒グラフ、円グラフ、折れ線グラフ、イラストなどが含まれます。地図や平面図の場合、現在の居場所や目的地はどこなのか、音声に集中しながら聞きましょう。

Questions 7-9 🔊 34

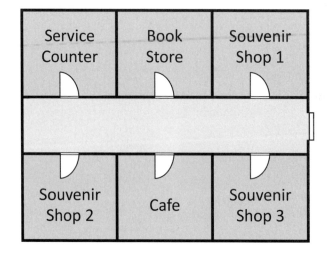

7. What did the man do this morning?
   (A) Took an airplane
   (B) Visited a memorial park
   (C) Installed some new software
   (D) Found a red tablet

8. According to the man, what was in the bag?
   (A) A red charm
   (B) A brown bear
   (C) A battery charger
   (D) A souvenir

9. Look at the graphic. Where did the man lose his bag?
   (A) Service counter
   (B) Book store
   (C) Souvenir shop 1
   (D) Souvenir shop 2

## Part 4　Talks

Questions 10-12　　🔊 35

**10.** Where is the announcement probably being made?

(A) On a bus

(B) On a train

(C) At a station

(D) At an airport

**11.** What are the listeners advised to do at the next stop?

(A) Change to another train

(B) Check the timetable

(C) Follow instructions by the staff

(D) Get a refund

**12.** How can the listeners receive a meal voucher?

(A) By booking a seat online

(B) By giving the staff their ticket

(C) By visiting any restaurant

(D) By purchasing a round-trip ticket

**Part 5** Incomplete Sentences

**Strategy for Part 5** ［短文穴埋め問題の解き方］

動詞の形問題 ③ 「自動詞」と「他動詞」

☆「自動詞」って何？

「自動詞」は目的語を必要としない動詞です。つまり直後に名詞を置くことができません。

※自動詞は目的語をとらないので受動態にはなりません。

☆「他動詞」って何？

「他動詞」は目的語を必要とする動詞です。直後に目的語となる名詞などが続きます。例えば、他動詞
marry（～と結婚する）の目的語は「結婚する相手」です。

「ウェンデルはローラと結婚する」は、

◎ Wendell will marry Laura. です。

× Wendell will marry. のように、目的語なしで使うことはできません。

また、日本語の感覚で（～と結婚する）

× Wendell will marry with Laura.

のように、前置詞を入れることはできません。

13. Everyone needs to come to the office so we can ------- ways to clean up the bus terminal.

    (A) discuss　　　　(B) discuss about　(C) look　　　　　(D) look about

14. The crew of the airline will meet this afternoon to ------- the boarding procedure.

    (A) tell　　　　　(B) tell about　　　(C) talk　　　　　(D) talk about

15. It appears ------- a bit too soon to promote him to the ground-staff manager's position.

    (A) that　　　　　(B) to be　　　　　(C) like　　　　　(D) to do

16. When you ------- the station, please let me know immediately.

    (A) reach　　　　(B) arrive　　　　(C) get　　　　　　(D) stop

# Part 6　Text Completion

Questions 17-20 refer to the following advertisement.

---

**Spend Your Winter Holidays Exploring Tropical Islands!**

Have you decided on your plans for the winter holidays yet? For those of you who are tired of staying home in the cold weather, Midwell Travel would like to offer you a tour of the tropical Matomba Islands. -------. For example, the beautiful unspoilt sea
**17.**
around the islands cannot be described! To further understand the islands' natural environment and how it has been preserved for so long, the tour includes some unique activities, such as a walking trip through the jungle. Sounds scary? No worries, ------- tour guides, who are familiar with the area, will be with you and will explain
**18.**
some of the environmental work that has been going on. Why don't you enjoy -------
**19.**
on these wonderfully preserved nature islands, while ------- a deeper understanding of
**20.**
this unique place this winter?

---

**17.** (A) The number of visitors has been increasing.

　　 (B) Please make sure you have received the itinerary.

　　 (C) They are the fruits of many years of environmental preservation.

　　 (D) The details of the tour have not been fixed yet.

**18.** (A) certified　　　(B) certify　　　(C) certification　　　(D) certifying

**19.** (A) you　　　(B) yours　　　(C) yourself　　　(D) your

**20.** (A) gaining　　　(B) gains　　　(C) will gain　　　(D) have gained

**Part 7** Single Passages / Multiple Passages

**Strategy for Part 7** ［読解問題の解き方］

**トリプル・パッセージ型**

　Part 7 の最後、設問 186 から設問 200 までは、3 つの文書を読んで解答する設問が 5 問ずつ 3 セット出題されます。いわゆる「トリプル・パッセージ型」ですが、「ダブル・パッセージ型」よりもさらに文書量が多く、またリーディングセクションの最後ということもあり、何となく難しく見え、最初から解くことをあきらめてはいませんか。

　リーディングセクション全体の解答時間は 75 分と非常に限られているので、これら 15 問すべてを解くとなると、時間が足りないのはやむをえないかもしれません。しかし、「トリプル・パッセージ型」の設問自は決して難問ばかりではないのです。

　まずは、それぞれのパッセージの「つながり」を意識して読んでみましょう（例：求人広告 ⇒ 応募者からのメール ⇒ 求人側からの結果のお知らせ）。3 つの文書から全体の「ストーリー」が見えてくれば、解ける問題も増えていくはずです。

Questions 21-25 refer to the following Web pages and e-mail.

---

http://www.nasunovillage.or.jp ☆

### ~ *SHIGATSUDO (Confectionary Shop)* ~

NASUNO Area, which has been an area blessed with abundant pure water and a moderate climate, is well-known for the production of high-quality rice in this country. Ever since Shozaemon Higashi established his first shop in 1853, they have been producing the finest confectionaries, such as their signature "Moon in Spring" rice cake.

The shop is open from 10:00 A.M. to 3:00 P.M on weekdays but closes earlier if the confectionaries sell out. Visitors to their factory are welcome during its business hours, unless it is too busy. On Saturdays, a workshop is held in the factory offering up to five visitors a chance to make with their pastry chefs. Why don't you experience the world of traditional Japanese confectionary? For further information, please visit the Web site at www.shigatsudo.co.jp.

http://www.sweetsworld.com ☆

## The Fusion of Traditional and Modern Tastes

*SHIGATSUDO, Nasuno Village*
*– "We were touched by their craftsmanship! We've never had such beautiful and tasty sweets in our life. We highly recommend any of their products, especially the 'Moon in Spring', which is also introduced on the Nasuno Village Web site. It was lucky for us to have a chance to attend a workshop by the company's head pastry chef, Takashi Yokota. We were very impressed with his outstanding skills and his unparalleled enthusiasm for confectionaries.*

 *Both the shop and the factory are only 5 minutes' walk from Nasuno Station and easy to find. Please note that there are very few trains to Nasuno, so you may want to check the timetable beforehand." –*

*– Sarah and Tony Sinclair (Manchester, UK)*

| To: | Sarah Sinclair <sarah.sinclair@comnet.com> |
|---|---|
| From: | Editorial Department <editorial@burleightraval.co.uk> |
| Subject: | FW: Request for permission |
| Date: | 21 May |

Dear Mr. and Mrs. Sinclair,

Thank you very much for writing your review on our Web site 'Sweets World'. We are forwarding the following e-mail we received from the Nasuno Village Office in Japan yesterday.

Kind regards
Burleigh Travel Co., Ltd.

------------------------------------------------------------------------------------

Dear Mr. and Mrs. Sinclair,

Thank you very much for visiting Nasuno Village last month. One of my colleagues happened to find your comment on 'Sweets World' a few days ago. We are happy to hear that you had a great time at SHIGATSUDO confectionary shop. How was your first experience of making Japanese sweets and pastries?

Since your comments and the photos of you working with Mr. Yokota on the Web site are very impressive, we would appreciate it if you would kindly allow us to post your positive review and wonderful photos on the village Web site.

We look forward to hearing from you soon.

Kind regards,
Shane Morita,
International Promotion staff, Nasuno Village Office

21. According to the first Web page, what is mentioned about the area?
    (A) It has been producing a variety of local specialties.
    (B) There are a large number of foreign visitors.
    (C) It is famous for its production of superior grain.
    (D) Its picturesque views are often introduced in guidebooks.

22. According to the second Web page, what is most likely true about the shop?
    (A) It is advertised by the village.
    (B) It is easy to find in the village.
    (C) It is closed on weekends.
    (D) It is a family-owned business.

23. On the second Web page, the word "unparalleled" in paragraph 1, line 6, is closest in meaning to
    (A) outstanding
    (B) predicted
    (C) challenging
    (D) exclusive

**24.** What is suggested about Mr. and Mrs. Sinclair?

(A) They lost their way to the shop.

(B) They stayed near the station.

(C) They visited the village in April.

(D) They joined the factory tour.

**25.** What is implied about Ms. Morita?

(A) She has lived in the area for many years.

(B) She did not know Mr. and Mrs. Sinclair's contact details.

(C) She has a friend working for the shop as a chef.

(D) She regularly researches the confectionary industry.

UNIT **8**
**Housing**

## Vocabulary Check!

Choose an appropriate translation for the following words.

🔊 36

| | | |
|---|---|---|
| **1.** prominently ( ) | **2.** renovation ( ) | **3.** assistance ( ) |
| **4.** state-of-the-art ( ) | **5.** sewage ( ) | **6.** committee ( ) |
| **7.** exclusive ( ) | **8.** transplant ( ) | **9.** delay ( ) |
| **10.** property ( ) | **11.** thoroughly ( ) | **12.** landscape ( ) |

| | | | |
|---|---|---|---|
| a. 完全に | b. 遅延 | c. 移植 | d. 財産 |
| e. 風景 | f. 委員会 | g. 傑出して | h. 改修 |
| i. 独占的な | j. 下水 | k. 支援 | l. 最新の |

## 🎧 Listening Section

### Part 1　Photographs

#### Strategy for Part 1 ［写真描写問題の解き方］

**風景、室内の写真 ③**

　Part 1 全体にわたって、選択肢は「現在形」や「現在進行形」になっていることがほとんどです。前のユニットで学習した、風景、室内の写真では現在完了形の受動態「has / have+been+ 過去分詞」を含む選択肢が出現する、ということと併せて、時制に着目しながら練習してみましょう。

**1.**

Ⓐ Ⓑ Ⓒ Ⓓ

**2.**　🔊 37

Ⓐ Ⓑ Ⓒ Ⓓ

### Part 2　Question-Response

#### Strategy for Part 2 ［応答問題の解き方］

**依頼・許可・提案・勧誘 ①　Can you ~ ?, May I ~ ?**

　Can you ~ ?, May I ~ ? で始まる表現は直訳すると、「~できますか」「~してもいいですか」ですが、単純に相手ができるかどうか、自分がしてもよいかを答える選択肢だけが正解ではなく、「~していただけますか」「~をしようと思っています」などのニュアンスで、ナチュラルな「依頼」や「許可」を表しています。会話が流れているものを選びましょう。

🔊 38

**3.**　Mark your answer on your answer sheet.　Ⓐ Ⓑ Ⓒ

**4.**　Mark your answer on your answer sheet.　Ⓐ Ⓑ Ⓒ

**5.**　Mark your answer on your answer sheet.　Ⓐ Ⓑ Ⓒ

**6.**　Mark your answer on your answer sheet.　Ⓐ Ⓑ Ⓒ

Questions 7-9　　　　　　　　　　　　　　　　　　　🔊 39

7.　What did the man probably do recently?

(A) He wondered about the office.

(B) He borrowed a huge desk.

(C) He ordered his favorite dish.

(D) He moved to a new space.

8.　What does the man want the woman to do?

(A) To find a new apartment

(B) To look into the incidence

(C) To arrange the layout of his room

(D) To set the table for dinner

9.　What is the woman planning to do tomorrow morning?

(A) She will buy a table.

(B) She will get some medicine.

(C) She will make a plan.

(D) She will arrive earlier than usual.

## Part 4　Talks

Questions 10-12　　🔊 40

**10.** Where is the announcement most likely taking place?

(A) In the entrance hall

(B) In a conference room

(C) In the factory

(D) In the yard

**11.** According to the speaker, what is the main feature of the new facility?

(A) It is equipped with advanced technologies.

(B) It is made of natural resources.

(C) It is surrounded by forests.

(D) It is more spacious than the old one.

**12.** What does the speaker imply when she says, "we have the conference hall all day"?

(A) The conference is anticipated to last long.

(B) The weather is reported to get worse.

(C) The outdoor event can be rescheduled.

(D) The hall is exclusive to company executives.

**Part 5** Incomplete Sentences

**Strategy for Part 5** ［短文穴埋め問題の解き方］

文法問題 ③　関係代名詞

　Part 5 には「関係代名詞」と「関係副詞」の両方が並ぶ問題がよく出題されます。

**関係代名詞**は「接続詞」と「代名詞」両方の働きをする。

**関係副詞**は「接続詞」と「副詞」両方の働きをする。

　このユニットでは「関係代名詞」を、次のユニットで「関係副詞」を学びましょう。

☆「**関係代名詞**」

関係代名詞は「接続詞」と同じように、2 つの文をつないで 1 つの文にする働きがあり、「（代）名詞」のように導く節で主語や目的語になります。

| 先行詞 | 主格 | 所有格 | 目的格 |
|--------|------|--------|--------|
| 人 | who | whose | whom |
| 事物 | which | whose | which |
| 人・事物 | that | — | that |

**13.** I can't find the house ------- I want to look around.

    (A) where     (B) whose     (C) which     (D) who

**14.** ------- he possesses is the talent to get straight to the core of a problem and solve it.

    (A) That     (B) What     (C) When     (D) Where

**15.** I love this room. I will do ------- I have to do to purchase it.

    (A) whoever     (B) whatever     (C) whenever     (D) wherever

**16.** This is the reason for ------- the husband chose this timber.

    (A) when     (B) why     (C) what     (D) which

## Part 6　Text Completion

**Strategy for Part 6**［長文穴埋め問題の解き方］

**必要な文法力 ①**

　TOEIC L&R では、どのくらいのレベルの英文法が要求されるのでしょうか。確かにリーディングセクション、特に Part 5 と Part 6 では一定の文法力が必要です。そして残念ながら、「中学や高校で習った英文法をあまり覚えていない」などという理由で、TOEIC L&R にも苦手意識を持ってしまう人は少なくないようです。

　そこで、夏休みや春休みなど、まとまった時間がある時に、**中学英文法の問題集を 1 冊終わらせてみては**いかがでしょう。遠回りに思えるかもしれませんが、「中学校で学ぶレベルの英文法は必須」の TOEIC L&R では、一定レベルの英文法を身につけておくと、後々スコアの伸びが速くなります。文法は、皆さんの心強い「味方」になってくれるはずです。

Questions 17-20 refer to the following article.

### The Renewed Central Library

According to the town hall, the remodeling of the Central Library has been finally completed, and it will be reopened on June 25.

-------. However, it was delayed due to several revisions to the original plan. When
　17.
the original plan was announced by the previous mayor, there were a lot of complaints and suggestions from local residents, especially about the extension. Then, the details of the plan were ------- reviewed in every aspect, with various
　　　　　　　　　　　　　　　　　　　18.
people, ranging from constructors to botanists. About a month ------- schedule,
　　　　　　　　　　　　　　　　　　　　　　　　　　19.
the revised plan ------- by the city council on March 7, and then, a tender for
　　　　　　　　　20.
construction was placed the following month.

17. (A) The renovation was supposed to be finished in May.
　　(B) A press conference was not held in the renewed building.
　　(C) Town officials apologized for their misunderstanding.
　　(D) Most local people were concerned about its location.

18. (A) prominently　　(B) approximately　(C) thoroughly　　(D) apparently

19. (A) behind　　　　(B) before　　　　(C) on　　　　　(D) as

20. (A) is being approved
　　(B) will be approved
　　(C) was approved
　　(D) approved

Questions 21-25 refer to the following text-message chain.

---

**Allison Wells (10:12 A.M.)** Hi, everyone. You've heard that our apartment building will be having a periodic checkup on May 24, haven't you?

**Terry Brooks (10:13 A.M.)** Hi, Alison, thank you for taking good care of our apartments as always. Yes, I've heard that.

**Mina Stewart (10:14 A.M.)** Will it? Is there anything we have to do in advance?

**Allison Wells (10:15 A.M.)** Not at all. Some inspection equipment may be placed in the corridors, but we will have nothing to do during the inspection.

**Terry Brooks (10:16 A.M.)** Allison, do you think the inspectors will point out any problems with this building?

**Allison Wells (10:17 A.M.)** Unfortunately, I think they will, because I've recently received a lot of complaints about its facilities, such as water leaks, cracks in the floors, and elevator breakdowns, from some of the residents.

**Mina Stewart (10:18 A.M.)** I'd agree to some renovations, but I am worried about how much they will cost.

**Terry Brooks (10:19 A.M.)** Me too. I guess that the inspector will recommend replacing the sewage pipes and water-proofing the roof at least.

**Allison Wells (10:20 A.M.)** Yes, and there could be more than that. Why don't we organize a renovation planning committee to discuss the issues?

---

21. What most likely did the residents receive?

(A) Notification of an event

(B) Requests for assistance

(C) Announcement of a meeting

(D) Estimated price of a property

22. What is the group concerned about?

(A) Water leaks

(B) Elevator malfunctions

(C) Repair cost

(D) Floor damage

23. What is suggested about the upcoming event?

(A) It is irregularly held in the apartment block.

(B) It may be harder to walk through the hallways.

(C) The residents will need to prepare for it.

(D) A meeting will be called before the event.

24. At 10:14 A.M., what does Ms. Stewart mean when she writes, "Will it"?

(A) She is surprised at changes in the apartment's policy.

(B) She wants to confirm the meeting schedule.

(C) She did not know about the building inspection.

(D) She has not heard about the renovation committee plans.

25. What is most likely true about Ms. Wells?

(A) She is the building manager of the apartment.

(B) She was supposed to inspect the property.

(C) She has asked some constructors for an estimate.

(D) She will be chairing the new committee.

## Vocabulary Check!

Choose an appropriate translation for the following words.

🔊 41

| | | |
|---|---|---|
| **1.** orchestra ( ) | **2.** audience ( ) | **3.** countless ( ) |
| **4.** ballot ( ) | **5.** temporary ( ) | **6.** row ( ) |
| **7.** energetic ( ) | **8.** obscure ( ) | **9.** transportation ( ) |
| **10.** agriculture ( ) | **11.** permission ( ) | **12.** masterpiece ( ) |

| | | | |
|---|---|---|---|
| a. 数えきれない | b. 列 | c. 聴衆 | d. 投票 |
| e. あいまいな | f. 許可 | g. オーケストラ | h. 交通 |
| i. 農業 | j. 代表作 | k. 熱意のある | l. 一時的な |

# 🎧 Listening Section

## Part 1　Photographs

**Strategy for Part 1 ［写真描写問題の解き方］**

複数人物の写真④

　複数人物が写真に写っていて、その主語が周辺のものや、主語が注目したり身につけたりしているものであるときには、その主語は 4 つの選択肢すべてにおいて異なることが多いです。それぞれの主語、動詞、それに続く修飾語句がすべて一致しているかについてチェックしながら正解を選びましょう。

**1.**

Ⓐ Ⓑ Ⓒ Ⓓ

**2.** 🔊 42

Ⓐ Ⓑ Ⓒ Ⓓ

## Part 2　Question-Response

**Strategy for Part 2 ［応答問題の解き方］**

依頼・許可・提案・勧誘 ②　Why don't you ~ ?

　Why don't you ~ ? で始まる表現は直訳すると「どうして~しないの？」ですが、要するに「~してもよいのではないですか？（どうしていけないのか？）」のニュアンスで、「提案」や「勧誘」を表しています。

🔊 43

**3.**　Mark your answer on your answer sheet.　Ⓐ Ⓑ Ⓒ

**4.**　Mark your answer on your answer sheet.　Ⓐ Ⓑ Ⓒ

**5.**　Mark your answer on your answer sheet.　Ⓐ Ⓑ Ⓒ

**6.**　Mark your answer on your answer sheet.　Ⓐ Ⓑ Ⓒ

**Strategy for Part 3**［会話問題の解き方］

**2 人の会話問題 ③**

Part 3 の設問の先読みと同時に、似ている選択肢が並ぶパターンを攻略しておきましょう。例えば、選択肢に

(A) At 8:00 A.M.

(B) At 10:30 A.M.

(C) At 11:30 A.M.

(D) At 11:30 A.M.

と並んでいたら、選択肢を見ただけで時間を聞かれていることが明らかです。そしてさらに設問から、何が起こるかについてポイントを絞ることができるでしょう。

Questions 7-9 　　　　　　　　　　　　　　　　　　　　　🔊 44

7. What are the speakers discussing?

(A) The restaurant's location

(B) Customers' complaints

(C) The menu for dinner

(D) The plan for this afternoon

8. What are they planning to do before the show?

(A) Leave the auditorium

(B) Eat at the cafeteria

(C) Prepare for the audio

(D) Wait at the entrance

9. What time does the show begin?

(A) At noon

(B) At 1 o'clock

(C) Before 2 P.M.

(D) After 2 P.M.

## Part 4　Talks

Questions 10-12　🔊 45

10. What will happen to Leicester Theater in a few weeks?
    (A) It will be expanded.
    (B) It will be relocated.
    (C) It will have another building.
    (D) It will start selling tickets.

11. What will the listeners newly find on the 23 November?
    (A) Some box seats
    (B) Some studios
    (C) A souvenir shop
    (D) A wheelchair ramp

12. What member's information is required online?
    (A) A phone number
    (B) An e-mail address
    (C) A postal code
    (D) An ID number

**Part 5** Incomplete Sentences

**Strategy for Part 5** ［短文穴埋め問題の解き方］

文法問題 ④　関係副詞

　関係副詞は「接続詞」と同じように 2 つの文をつないで 1 つの文にする働きがあり、 導く節の中で、「副詞」の役割をします。単なる副詞として考えられるので、この副詞がなくても文として成立します。

| 関係副詞 | 先行詞の例（省略できる） | |
|---|---|---|
| 時 when | the time, day | The manager wants to know (the time) when you will come. |
| 場所 where | the place, the house | The airport was (the place) where I met George. |
| 理由 why | the reason | I don't know (the reason) why she is absent today. |
| 方法 how | ※ the way | That's how they entered the house.<br>=That's the way they entered the house. |

※ the way how ～ はありません。（how は先行詞と一緒に用いない）

13. Please explain ------- the concert was canceled.
    (A) where　　　　(B) why　　　　(C) date　　　　(D) the hall

14. ------- practices hard for the show, will succeed.
    (A) Whatever　　(B) No matter　　(C) However　　(D) Whoever

15. Used uniforms can be brought directly to the front desk ------- the cleaning staff will take care of them.
    (A) which　　　　(B) where　　　　(C) there　　　　(D) why

16. Let me know the date ------- you want to see the movie.
    (A) when　　　　(B) where　　　　(C) who　　　　(D) where

## Part 6　Text Completion

**Strategy for Part 6**［長文穴埋め問題の解き方］

**語彙の増やし方①**

　Unit 7 で紹介した Part 6 の設問の種類のうち、「2. 文脈に沿って解く設問」の1つ**「語彙を選ぶ問題（通称・語彙問題）」**は、Part 6 全16問中、2～4問程度出題されます。「語彙問題」の選択肢はすべて同じ品詞であり、文法で解くことはできません。よって前後の文脈から、意味的に最もふさわしい単語を選びます。

　この際、選択肢にかなり難しい単語が入っていることがあります。このような場合、何となくそれが正解に見えてしまうことはありませんか。しかし、このような選択肢は**不正解を誘う「誤答選択肢（destructor）」**であることが多いようです。

　ボキャブラリーを増やす時はまず、基本的な語句から取り組んでみてください。難しい語句はその後で構いません。もちろん語彙は多い方がよいでしょうが、文書を読めるかどうかはたいてい、初級から中級レベルの語句を知っているかどうかで決まります。

Questions 17-20 refer to the following advertisement.

---

### The Musical 'Mother and Daughter' is Coming Back!

Sun Star Music Co., Ltd. is pleased to inform you that 'Mother and Daughter' will be finally staged again by Theater Clocks from February 1. The famous musical, which has been loved ------- the generations, will be performed by a completely new cast. -------. This **17.** **18.** time, Theater Clocks will have a nationwide tour of this timeless masterpiece, starting from ------- hometown, Gatwick City. **19.**

To celebrate the ------- of the musical, there is a special event. After each play finishes, **20.** 10 lucky audience members will be allowed to take pictures and talk with the actors and actresses backstage for free! To apply for your chance to go backstage, please check the box 'Apply for the special event' when you purchase your ticket online.

---

**17.** (A) across　　　(B) within　　　(C) during　　　(D) into

**18.** (A) However, we regret to tell you that all tickets have been sold.
　　(B) Reviews from audiences are now available on our Web site.
　　(C) A list of members will be unveiled at tomorrow's press conference.
　　(D) The hall accommodates an audience of over five thousand.

**19.** (A) it　　　(B) its　　　(C) them　　　(D) they

**20.** (A) revitalization　　(B) reduction　　(C) revival　　(D) reluctance

**Strategy for Part 7** ［読解問題の解き方］

設問パターン⑤

　Unit 2 で紹介した Part 7 の設問の種類のうち、**6. 単語の意味を問うタイプ（通称・同義語問題）**は、Part 7 全 54 問中、多くて 5 問程度出題されます。

　問われている語がある場所は「○段落・×行目」のように設問に明記されており、解答にあまり時間はかかりません。よって、このタイプの設問は、テストの残り時間が少ない時でもぜひ解いてみてください。また、単語単体で同じ意味を持つ選択肢を見つけたとしても、**実際に設問の単語と置き換えてみて、文脈に当てはまるかどうかまで確認してください。**

　新しい単語を覚える際は、類義語もチェックし、まとめて覚えることも有効な方法です。

Questions 21-25 refer to the following Web page.

### Why don't you help us liven up our city festival?

Why don't we make our city's annual event the most successful yet? The Executive Committee of the well-known Darling Film Festival is seeking 20 energetic staff members for our 12th Festival.

Since the first film festival was held here in Darling City, a countless number of local people have been devoted to supporting the festivals as staff members in various ways. Some of them advertised our events in the media and negotiated permission to use the city's convention hall with city officials. Others asked renowned film directors to enter the competition, and even operated shuttles between the venue and the station on the day of the event.

Staff members will be paid, receive free meals and be offered refreshments during the festival and, especially for this year ... complimentary tickets for special seats available when you are off-duty!

You can now apply for positions on our Web site no later than August 5. Please make sure to upload your résumé and a recent photo for your application. Short-listed candidates will be contacted by e-mail regarding an interview by August 17.

**21.** What is the purpose of the Web page?

(A) To notify a ballot result

(B) To promote a movie theater

(C) To invite directors to a convention

(D) To recruit staff for an event

**22.** The word "renowned" in paragraph 2, line 4, is closest in meaning to

(A) awarded    (B) eminent    (C) obscure    (D) freelanced

**23.** What did the previous staff NOT do?

(A) Meet with the city officials

(B) Provide transportation services

(C) Advertise the festival

(D) Cater to the guests

**24.** What will the staff members be offered during the event?

(A) A backstage pass    (B) An ID tag

(C) Light meals    (D) Bus tickets

**25.** What is suggested about the Executive Committee?

(A) It has been allocated a sufficient budget.

(B) It will interview some of the applicants.

(C) It consists of local residents.

(D) It belongs to the city office.

UNIT **10**
Hobby

## Vocabulary Check!

Choose an appropriate translation for the following words.

🔊 46

| | | |
|---|---|---|
| **1.** competition ( ) | **2.** procedure ( ) | **3.** architecture ( ) |
| **4.** historian ( ) | **5.** relocate ( ) | **6.** pottery ( ) |
| **7.** sculpture ( ) | **8.** campaign ( ) | **9.** trim ( ) |
| **10.** cart ( ) | **11.** attach ( ) | **12.** fabulous ( ) |

| | | | |
|---|---|---|---|
| a. 場所を変更する | b. 手続き | c. 陶磁器 | d. くっつける |
| e. 刈る | f. キャンペーン | g. カート | h. すばらしい |
| i. 建築物 | j. 歴史家 | k. 競争 | l. 彫刻 |

# 🎧 Listening Section

## Part 1　Photographs

1.

2.　　🔊 47

Ⓐ　Ⓑ　Ⓒ　Ⓓ

Ⓐ　Ⓑ　Ⓒ　Ⓓ

## Part 2　Question-Response

🔊 48

3.　Mark your answer on your answer sheet.　　Ⓐ　Ⓑ　Ⓒ

4.　Mark your answer on your answer sheet.　　Ⓐ　Ⓑ　Ⓒ

5.　Mark your answer on your answer sheet.　　Ⓐ　Ⓑ　Ⓒ

6.　Mark your answer on your answer sheet.　　Ⓐ　Ⓑ　Ⓒ

**Strategy for Part 3** [会話問題の解き方]

**2 人の会話問題 ④**

　Part 3 では、音声の流れる順番に設問を解くヒントが出てくることが多いので、設問はほぼ上から順番に解くことができます。先読みが十分にできない場合でも、3 問セットの問題の 1 問目から解答するつもりで、音声を聞きながら集中して解きましょう。

Questions 7-9　　　　　　　　　　　　　　　　　　　　　　　🔊 49

7.　What is this conversation about?

　　(A) A sales report

　　(B) Architecture

　　(C) A defense method

　　(D) A classic concert

8.　What was the woman's problem when the tickets went on sale?

　　(A) The volume was too low.

　　(B) The client was not there.

　　(C) The connection was not stable.

　　(D) The bank was closed.

9.　What does the man suggest to the woman?

　　(A) To go to another concert

　　(B) To look for a piano

　　(C) To find a better wi-fi connection

　　(D) To go to the second floor

## Part 4  Talks

Questions 10-12                                              🔊 50

**10.** When will the event finish?

(A) On February 18

(B) On February 19

(C) On February 22

(D) On February 23

**11.** Who is Scott Bennett?

(A) An artist

(B) A printer

(C) A mayor

(D) A historian

**12.** According to the speaker, what will Ann McCarthy do?

(A) Guide visitors around the museum

(B) Explain details of the artworks

(C) Introduce a history of the city

(D) Present information on future events

## Part 5 Incomplete Sentences

### Strategy for Part 5 ［短文穴埋め問題の解き方］

文法問題 ⑤　比較級

比較級：2 つのものを比べて「もっと～、より～」という意味を表す。

☆「比較級」の問題でよく出題されるパターン

① 比較級 +than（文中に than があり、空所に比較級を選ぶパターンで頻出）

1 音節の短い形容詞には形容詞の後に -er をつけて比較級の表現とします。

My mother is taller than my sister. 「母は私の姉より背が高い」

② more+〈形容詞の原級／副詞の原級〉+than（〈more+ 原級〉を選択肢から選ぶパターンで出現）

主に比較級となる形容詞、副詞の綴りが長い場合（2 音節以上）

That watch is more expensive than this one. 「あの腕時計はこちらよりも高価だ」

③ the+ 比較級 +S+V, the+ 比較級 +S+V　（比較級の部分が空所になっていることが多い）

「…すればするほどますます～」の意味です。

The older we get, the more considerate we become.

「年を取れば取るほど、我々はより思慮深くなる」

13. Our new golf club is ------- than our competitor's new release.

    (A) more reasonable          (B) more efficiently

    (C) as reasonable             (D) as efficient

14. The first test result seems to be the ------- of the two that George took for his job application.

    (A) great        (B) better        (C) well        (D) bigger

15. Please send us a box of books. We need to get them as quickly -------.

    (A) as good        (B) as possible        (C) very fast        (D) better

16. Infectious diseases were spread ------- in the past than today partly because of the people's lack of awareness about hygiene.

    (A) quick        (B) quickly        (C) more quickly        (D) the most quickly

## Part 6　Text Completion

Questions 17-20 refer to the following notice.

Highbury Town Annual Art Competition

The Highbury Art Museum is pleased to announce that the 15th City Art Competition will be held on April 7 as scheduled. Having had our budget reduced due to the unexpected repair works of the main building, we launched a crowdfunding campaign for the first time. -------. We express our deepest gratitude
**17.**
to the fundraisers. Without their cooperation, we ------- the competition this year.
**18.**

The competition will be divided into three categories; paintings, sculptures and pottery pieces. ------- amateurs or professionals, every citizen is eligible to
**19.**
participate in the competition. The ------- of the application process are now
**20.**
available on the Web site. We look forward to your finest artworks.

17. (A) Fortunately, it resulted in a huge success.
    (B) Meanwhile, we had to increase the admission fee.
    (C) Therefore, we cannot expect so many participants.
    (D) Accordingly, there will be fewer sponsors this year.

18. (A) cannot have held　　　　　　(B) cannot be held
    (C) could not hold　　　　　　　(D) could not be held

19. (A) Whether　　(B) Either　　(C) Whichever　　(D) Otherwise

20. (A) detail　　(B) details　　(C) detailed　　(D) detailing

---

**Strategy for Part 7 ［読解問題の解き方］**

設問パターン ⑥

　Unit 2 で紹介した Part 7 の設問のうちの **7. 文が入る位置を問うタイプ**を難しく感じる受験者は多いようです。では、なぜ難しいと感じるのでしょうか。

　設問にある文、いわゆる「挿入文」が入る位置を見つけるためには、挿入文中にある①代名詞や、②「つなぎ言葉（接続副詞など）」などが参考になります。①代名詞とは、前に出てきた人物や物事を置き換えるもの、②「つなぎ言葉」とは、前に書いてある内容との関係を示すものですね。

　しかし、「前に」あるものを突き止めるためには…結局、文書全体の内容（あらすじ・ストーリー）を把握する必要があるのです。Part 7 の 54 問中 2 問しか出題されないこのタイプの設問ですが、これも 2016 年 TOEIC が新しくなった際に加わりました。この改定の主な目的の 1 つは、**「文書の一部だけ読めば解けるような設問を減らし、文書をすべて読まなければ解けない問題を増やすこと」**にあると考えられています。つまり、「設問そのものが難しい」というより、「『読む力』を持たずに解くことが難しい」のかもしれません。

---

Questions 21-25 refer to the following advertisement and online form.

---

### Eric's Dance School Opening New Studio

Don't you want to dance to your favorite music? If so, Eric's Dance School is for you. We will be opening our new dance studio in Preston at the beginning of September. The studio will have state-of-the-art equipment and be twice as large as the studio at our main school.

There will be three categories of courses available by our fabulous instructors, Hip-hop, Jazz and Ballet. Students will be allocated according to their preferences and dance skills. All you need to do to enrol is fill out the application form below and click the 'Send' button. Please note, if you are new to us, you also need to take and send us a short video of one of your dance routines for us to decide which course will be best for you.

Once your course is decided, we will e-mail you further information about tuition fees, our bank transfer procedure and timetables.

Thank you.

---

| Name: | *Sally Rosenberg* | |
|---|---|---|
| Age: | *49* | |
| Address: | *118 Megan Road, Preston* | |
| Zip Code: | *95510 - 4043* | |
| Phone number: | (Home) *555 – 0118* | (Mobile) *0883 - 00224* |

| E-mail address: | sallyrosenberg@oliveline.com |
|---|---|
| Preferred Category: | *Jazz* |

Dancing Career: *I belonged to a dance club when I was a college student but have not danced much since then. Recently, my friend asked me to join her dance team to participate in a dance contest for seniors later this year and I've become eager to dance again. Please find attached the video of one of my dance routines.*

(Sent on September 20)

21. What is true about Eric's Dance School?
   (A) It has a variety of studios.
   (B) It has a small number of students.
   (C) It has been recently relocated.
   (D) It has up-to-date facilities.

22. What information is NOT required on the form?
   (A) Favorite music
   (B) Current address
   (C) Postal code
   (D) Mobile phone number

23. What are some of the applicants asked to do?
   (A) Attach a copy of their photo ID
   (B) Show a video of their performance
   (C) State their preferred course
   (D) Make a deposit for the tuition

24. What will Eric's Dance School most likely do for Ms. Rosenberg next?
   (A) Sign up for the contest
   (B) Decide her course
   (C) Send her an invoice
   (D) Contact an instructor

25. What is indicated about Ms. Rosenberg?
   (A) She has entered into a contest.
   (B) She has a career as a professional dancer.
   (C) She often dances for her health.
   (D) She lives in the same town as the school.

## Vocabulary Check!

Choose an appropriate translation for the following words. 🔊 51

| | | |
|---|---|---|
| **1.** enrollment (   ) | **2.** advisor (   ) | **3.** face-to-face (   ) |
| **4.** geometry (   ) | **5.** urgent (   ) | **6.** digitalization (   ) |
| **7.** contribute (   ) | **8.** pressroom (   ) | **9.** budget (   ) |
| **10.** specifically (   ) | **11.** innovative (   ) | **12.** certain (   ) |

| | | | |
|---|---|---|---|
| a. 印刷室 | b. 具体的に | c. ある、1つの | d. 予算 |
| e. デジタル化 | f. 対面の | g. 登録 | h. 幾何学 |
| i. 貢献する | j. 革新的な | k. アドバイスする人 | l. 急ぎの |

# 🎧 Listening Section

## Part 1 Photographs

### Strategy for Part 1 ［写真描写問題の解き方］

**写真問題のコツ ①**

　Part 1 では、4 つの選択肢の主語や、時制が一致していることが多く、リスニングをしながら、一定のリズムをつかむことができます。もし、わからない単語が出てきても、「主語」「動詞」「修飾語」のうちどの要素がわからないのかを認識すればわかる部分や、ほかの選択肢から消去法を使って回答することもできるでしょう。

**1.**

Ⓐ Ⓑ Ⓒ Ⓓ

**2.**　　🔊 52

Ⓐ Ⓑ Ⓒ Ⓓ

## Part 2 Question-Response

### Strategy for Part 2 ［応答問題の解き方］

**否定疑問文など ①　Don't ~ ?, Isn't ~ ? などで始まる否定疑問文**

　Don't you ~ ?, Aren't you ~ ?, Isn't he ~ ? などには「～でないの？」「私はこう思うんだけど、あなたは違うの？」というニュアンスが含まれます。多少の不満などの気持ちがある、とイメージしましょう。

🔊 53

**3.**　Mark your answer on your answer sheet.　　Ⓐ Ⓑ Ⓒ

**4.**　Mark your answer on your answer sheet.　　Ⓐ Ⓑ Ⓒ

**5.**　Mark your answer on your answer sheet.　　Ⓐ Ⓑ Ⓒ

**6.**　Mark your answer on your answer sheet.　　Ⓐ Ⓑ Ⓒ

**Strategy for Part 3** ［会話問題の解き方］

**2 人 × 3 ターンの会話 ②**

　Part 3 の設問 3 問のそれぞれには傾向があり、最初の問題は会話全体に関する問題、2 番目は詳細に関する問題、3 問目は会話によって決定した事項やこれから起こることに関する問題であることが多いです。

Questions 7-9　　　　　　　　　　　　　　　　　　　🔊 54

7. When is this conversation probably taking place?

(A) On Tuesday

(B) On Wednesday

(C) On Thursday

(D) On Saturday

8. What does the man need the poster for?

(A) For a traffic campaign

(B) For a calendar

(C) For a conference

(D) For an election

9. According to the woman, where is the printing office located?

(A) On the 7th floor

(B) Next to the secretary's room

(C) Behind the next building

(D) At the conference venue

## Part 4 Talks

Questions 10-12

🔊 55

**10.** Where does the speaker most likely work?

(A) At a publishing company

(B) At a book shop

(C) At a national library

(D) At a language center

**11.** According to the speaker, what happened in 2002?

(A) The guest published a book.

(B) The guest started a new business.

(C) The guest won a prize.

(D) The guest completed the courses.

**12.** What does the speaker imply when he says, "I don't think I need to tell you about her contributions to us in detail here"?

(A) He will mention them later.

(B) He is running out of time.

(C) The people are not interested in them.

(D) The people already know a lot about them.

**Part 5** **Incomplete Sentences**

**Strategy for Part 5** ［短文穴埋め問題の解き方］

文法問題 ⑥　最上級

最上級：３つ以上のものを比べて「最も〜」の意味を表す。

☆「最上級」の表現のおさらい

① the+〈形容詞 +-est／副詞 +-est〉
　Nathan is the tallest in his class.
　「ネイサンはクラスの中で一番背が高い」

② the+〈most+ 形容詞の原級／most+ 副詞の原級〉
　That picture is the most expensive item in the shop.
　「あの絵画はその店で最も高価な商品です」

③ one of the+〈最上級 + 名詞の複数形〉
　This is one of the longest holidays I've ever had.
　「この休暇は私が今まででとった最も長い休暇の１つです」

**13.** Mrs. Williams is ------- teacher that I've ever met.

(A) the best　　　(B) the most　　　(C) as good as　　　(D) much better

**14.** The president says ------- is more important than the safety of our employees.

(A) everything　　　(B) anything　　　(C) nothing　　　(D) something

**15.** Heidi's Federation has grown to become the ------- largest student union in New York, after the Christopher's Club.

(A) two　　　(B) secondly　　　(C) second　　　(D) of two

**16.** Diane is the ------- qualified applicant for the teaching assistant position because of her communication skills.

(A) maximum　　　(B) most　　　(C) best　　　(D) top

## Part 6  Text Completion

**Strategy for Part 6** ［長文穴埋め問題の解き方］

**語彙の増やし方 ③**

　Unit 6 で紹介した Part 6 の設問「1. 文脈に関係なく解ける設問」のうち、**「品詞を選ぶ問題」「前置詞を選ぶ問題」**は、あまり多く出題されません。が、文脈全体を考える必要がなく、Part 5 対策で身につけた知識を利用し、空所の前後を見るだけで解答できるので、確実に正解したい問題です。

　まず、英語の品詞は大半が**「接尾辞（語尾）」で区別**できます。特に名詞、動詞、形容詞、副詞の４つについては、主な語尾を今すぐに覚えましょう。

　また、前置詞は前後の語と組み合わせて使われるもの。よってここでも「前置詞＋名詞」「動詞＋前置詞」、「形容詞＋前置詞」のように、TOEIC L&R に頻繁に出てくる単語同士を組み合わせ、**フレーズ（語句のかたまり）で覚える習慣**が大きく役立ちます。

　前置詞を選ぶ問題は、考えて解けるものではありません。テスト本番では、**「知っていれば解ける、知らなければ解けない」**と割り切るとよいでしょう。

Questions 17-20 refer to the following notice.

Spring Intensive Computer Course Offered

Morton College of Technology will offer local business owners, who want to promote the digitalization of their business, a selection of computer courses this spring. ------- **17.** your business is located in Morton Town, you are eligible to apply for a subsidy to attend the courses. -------. **18.** For example, the Web design courses will be ------- **19.** great help to make your company's or shop's Web site more attractive. For those of you who have a certain level of IT knowledge, programming courses will be opened.

For further information, please visit our Web site, www.morton.ac.ca. Most of the courses became full soon after our announcement last year, so we highly recommend you to submit your ------- early. **20.**

**17.** (A) Ever since　　(B) Whereas　　(C) As long as　　(D) Unless

**18.** (A) The tuition depends on the course you will take.
　　　(B) A variety of useful courses are available.
　　　(C) Some courses may be canceled due to low enrollment.
　　　(D) Each course consists of ten to twelve lectures.

**19.** (A) of　　　　　(B) as　　　　　(C) with　　　　　(D) to

**20.** (A) application　(B) cooperation　(C) attendance　(D) assistance

**Strategy for Part 7** ［読解問題の解き方］

**読むスピード**

　Part 7 対策で、皆さんの多くは「速く的確に文脈（ストーリー）を読み取る力」を望むのではないでしょうか。では、TOEIC L&R で具体的にどのくらいの読解スピードが求められるのか、考えたことはありますか。

　設問 200 番まで解き終えるには、まず平均**「150 語／分」**くらいは必要、理想は「180 語／分」で、音声にするとリスニングセクションの Part 3 や Part 4 でナレーターが話すスピードとちょうど同じくらいです。ちなみに英語ネイティヴの読解スピードは「およそ 350 語／分」です。

　制限時間の厳しい Part 7、**「解くスピード」**を速くすることは難しくとも、**「読むスピード」を速くす**ることはできます。Part 7 に出てくる文書はそれほど複雑な内容ではありません。しかも、似た内容の文書がよく見受けられます。「TOEIC 的なストーリー」に慣れてくると、皆さんの読解スピードはさらに上がることでしょう。

Questions 21-25 refer to the following e-mail.

| From: | Greg Tau <greg.tau@hillburyls.ac.ie> |
|---|---|
| To: | Andrew Peterson <andrew.peterson@hillburyls.ac.ie> |
| Date: | August 7 |
| Subject: | Urgent matters |

I am pleased to hear that Hillbury Language School has received a number of inquiries about our new online courses. Specifically, I am surprised that we have already received a number of requests for estimates from companies planning to enroll their recruits in some of our courses. That means there is a certain demand for online business English courses as we expected.

Considering the number of potential students, their level of language skills will vary. Therefore, at yesterday's staff meeting, we decided to divide the students into five to six groups according to their level. Naturally, having more groups means that we will need more instructors, who are familiar with providing online classes. Could you please begin posting job positions immediately, and, soon after we receive a sufficient number of applications, schedule face-to-face job interviews with the applicants?

Also, expecting increasing demand for our distance learning courses, I think we should hire a few full-time IT technicians rather than outsourcing the IT-related services as we do now. I would like you to discuss this within your department and decide if it is necessary and if so, how many we will need.

If you have any ideas on these urgent matters, please feel free to visit my office when I am in or e-mail me when I am away from the office so I could arrange an online meeting with you.

Regards,
Greg Tau, Online Course Director

21. What is the purpose of the e-mail?
    (A) To call a video conference
    (B) To request some assistance
    (C) To arrange job interviews
    (D) To inform of schedule changes

22. The word "potential" in paragraph 2, line 1, is closest in meaning to
    (A) promising     (B) motivated     (C) outstanding     (D) prospective

23. In which department does Mr. Peterson most likely work?
    (A) An IT department
    (B) An accounting department
    (C) A human resources department
    (D) A public relations department

24. What does Mr. Tau suggest doing?
    (A) Computerizing their hiring process
    (B) Enhancing their course contents
    (C) Estimating the budget for new facilities
    (D) Consider hiring some experts

25. What is NOT suggested about Hillbury Language School?
    (A) It will increase the number of employees.
    (B) It will have more applications than expected.
    (C) It specializes in providing online courses.
    (D) It does not have its own computer-related section.

UNIT **12**
Sports

## Vocabulary Check!

Choose an appropriate translation for the following words.

🔊 56

| | | |
|---|---|---|
| 1. spectator ( ) | 2. opponent ( ) | 3. generate ( ) |
| 4. environmental ( ) | 5. downhill ( ) | 6. brochure ( ) |
| 7. brave ( ) | 8. collaboration ( ) | 9. legendary ( ) |
| 10. astronomy ( ) | 11. achieve ( ) | 12. stadium ( ) |

| | | | |
|---|---|---|---|
| a. 下降して | b. 環境の | c. パンフレット | d. 伝説の |
| e. 対戦相手 | f. 見物人 | g. 野球場 | h. 達成する |
| i. 共同作業 | j. 天文学 | k. 勇敢な | l. 発生する |

## 🎧 Listening Section

### Part 1　Photographs

---

**Strategy for Part 1**［写真描写問題の解き方］

**写真問題のコツ ②**

リスニングの音声を聞いているときに写真にないものが出てきたら間違いだということはわかりますね。Part 1 では写真にあるものが音声に流れてきているけれども、それが誤答選択肢であるパターンが頻出します。写真に見えているからといって早とちりしないように注意して聞きましょう。

---

**1.**

Ⓐ Ⓑ Ⓒ Ⓓ

**2.** 🔊 57

Ⓐ Ⓑ Ⓒ Ⓓ

### Part 2　Question-Response

---

**Strategy for Part 2**［応答問題の解き方］

**否定疑問文など ②　付加疑問文**

設問の最後が、~ don't you?, ~ is it?, ~ isn't it? などで終わり、「ですよね？」「ではないですよね？」と確認するのが付加疑問文です。否定疑問文、付加疑問文の考え方は同じで、例えば Didn't you say ~ ?「言わなかったの？」に対して、「言った」なら Yes (I did).「言わなかった」なら No (I didn't). で答えます。

---

🔊 58

**3.**　Mark your answer on your answer sheet.　　Ⓐ Ⓑ Ⓒ

**4.**　Mark your answer on your answer sheet.　　Ⓐ Ⓑ Ⓒ

**5.**　Mark your answer on your answer sheet.　　Ⓐ Ⓑ Ⓒ

**6.**　Mark your answer on your answer sheet.　　Ⓐ Ⓑ Ⓒ

**Strategy for Part 3** ［会話問題の解き方］

**3人の会話 ②**

登場人物の男性または女性のどちらかが2人となる場合、先に設問を読んでおくことでどちらが複数なのか見分けることが可能です。設問にmenとあれば、男性が複数、womenとあれば女性が複数になるとわかります。

Questions 7-9                                                                🔊 59

7. Why is the woman worried about Donald?

   (A) His answer was wrong.

   (B) His blood pressure was low.

   (C) He cannot find his face mask.

   (D) He looks depressed.

8. What happened to Donald?

   (A) He lost several games.

   (B) He took a medical check.

   (C) He studied astronomy.

   (D) He changed his hair color.

9. What will the men probably do on the weekend?

   (A) Book an operation

   (B) See Mr. Thomas

   (C) Play at a tournament

   (D) Purchase some equipment

## Part 4 Talks

**Strategy for Part 4 ［説明文問題の解き方］**

各種トークの「展開」はほぼ決まっている！⑥

Part 4 でよく登場するトークに**「留守番電話のメッセージ（telephone message）」**があります。聞き手（the listener）が後でこのメッセージを聞く際、どんな情報が必要かを考えましょう。すると、この種類のトークの典型的な展開が見えてきます。まず、**「名乗る」**、次に**「電話の目的」を知らせる**…そして「ご連絡をお待ちしています」という**聞き手への依頼など**で**「締める」**と、非常にスタイルの決まったトークであることがわかりますね。よって、必然的にそのようなポイントをたずねる設問が多くなるのです。

Questions 10-12 🔊 60

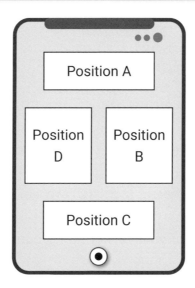

10. What is the speaker offering a trial with?

(A) A program

(B) A diet supplement

(C) A smartphone

(D) An online workshop

11. What most likely did the listener do recently?

(A) Contact a medical clinic

(B) Download a free app

(C) Report a problem

(D) E-mail an application form

12. Look at the graphic. Where will "Check My Health" appear on the screen?

(A) Position A

(B) Position B

(C) Position C

(D) Position D

## Part 5 Incomplete Sentences

### Strategy for Part 5 ［短文穴埋め問題の解き方］

文法問題 ⑦ 相関語句

☆相関語句のパターン

　接続語句の組み合わせの「相関語句」はよく出題されるので「決まり文句」として試験直前にも見直しておきましょう

| | |
|---|---|
| both A and B | 「A も B もどちらも」 |
| either A or B | 「A か B のどちらか」 |
| not only A but (also) B | 「A だけでなく B もまた」 |
| A as well as B | 「B だけでなく A も」 |
| not A but B | 「A ではなく B」 |
| neither A nor B | 「A も B も～ない」 |

13. Breakfast will be served until 10:00, you may choose ------- a buffet style or a restaurant style meal.

    (A) both　　　　　(B) either　　　　(C) two　　　　　(D) among

14. Keeping a good image of your racket swing benefits the movements of your arms and legs -------.

    (A) alike　　　　(B) both　　　　　(C) together　　　(D) all

15. The doctor emphasized the relationship ------- a good night's sleep and mental health.

    (A) on　　　　　(B) about　　　　(C) of　　　　　(D) between

16. He is not a professional golfer, ------- a weekend player.

    (A) but　　　　　(B) just as　　　　(C) also　　　　(D) although

## Part 6  Text Completion

**Strategy for Part 6** ［長文穴埋め問題の解き方］

**語彙の増やし方 ④**

　Unit 7 で紹介した Part 6 の設問「2. 文脈に沿って解く問題」のうち、**「文と文をつなぐ語句（接続副詞・つなぎ言葉）を選ぶ問題」**は、Part 6 全 16 問中、2、3 問程度出題されます。「前後をつなぐ」わけですから、空所を含む文の前後の文脈を考える必要があります。

　しかし、よく使われる「つなぎ言葉」はそれほど多くありません。10 〜 20 個程度ですので、まずは一通り覚えておくことをお勧めします。

　ちなみに、Writing でこれらの「つなぎ言葉」を使うと、皆さんの英文がよりフォーマルになります。TOEIC "L&R"（Listening & Reading）という名称のテストですが、工夫して活用すれば **Writing や Speaking に活かすことも**できます。そう考えると皆さんのモティベーションも上がりませんか。

Questions 17-20 refer to the following e-mail.

---

To: walter.bennett@globenet.com
From: customer@b-maxsports.com
Date: March 7
Subject: New aquatic center

Dear Mr. Bennett,

B-max Sports is pleased to inform you that our new aquatic center will be opened in Chelton next month. The center has three swimming pools, including a 50-meter-long one, ------- official competitions can be held, and a shallow one for young children. Also, the **17.** new building ------- attention for its state-of-the-art eco-friendly equipment. -------. For **18.** **19.** example, the 100 solar panels on the rooftop are expected to generate clean energy for most of the facilities.

Celebrating our grand opening of the center, we will offer our loyal members two-months free usage of any of the facilities. For further details, please visit our Web site.

Thank you very much for your ------- patronage. **20.**

Customer Support, B-max Sports

---

**17.** (A) where      (B) what        (C) which         (D) whose

**18.** (A) was drawn   (B) is drawing   (C) will be drawn   (D) have been drawing

**19.** (A) It is not conveniently located but surrounded by beautiful nature.

　　(B) Some of them will be completed behind schedule.

　　(C) It is designed based on our renewable energy sources policy.

　　(D) Environmental assessment will be conducted shortly by the town.

**20.** (A) continued     (B) continuation    (C) continual      (D) continuity

**Strategy for Part 7 [読解問題の解き方]**

**音声によるリーディング練習**

「公式 TOEIC L&R 問題集」や一部の TOEIC L&R 対策本には、英語ネイティヴ・スピーカーが Part 7 の文書を音読した音声ファイルが付属されるようになっています。リスニングではなくリーディングになぜ音声が付くのでしょうか。

実は速読の練習法として、「音声に合わせて、英文を目で追う」という方法が一般的になりつつあるのです。これを続けると、「英文を左から右に読む」くせがつきます。**結果的に右から左に戻る回数が減り、**読むスピードも上がるのです。また例えば「音声の再生スピードを上げ、英文を目で追うスピードも上げる」といったトレーニングも可能です。そもそも**英語は「左から右に」読み書きする言語**であることを忘れずに。

Questions 21-25 refer to the following article and online form.

Dartford (January 31) – Dartford City Football Club announced yesterday that its new "Arthur Stadium" has finally been completed. It was named after Arthur Reed, the legendary player for the club in the 19th century. Since the new stadium can accommodate over ten thousand spectators, the team is now eligible for promotion to the upper division if they achieve good results this season. "We will never forget what happened to us seven years ago." says, the president of the supporters club, Geoff Moore. "Our team was denied just because our stadium didn't meet the requirements of the league. It has been our earnest wish to build a bigger and better stadium ever since."

When the club, local businesses and the city signed the agreement for financing the new stadium in 2015, the construction project made a great step forward. "We fully agreed on the idea then," says, the then director of sports for the city, Sean McGregor, "and I am honored to deliver the opening remarks as mayor on the very first day for the new stadium. Hopefully, the new stadium will be a symbol of the collaboration of all the people who love our team and our city."

Dartford City F.C. will be holding the opening ceremony on February 11. Then, a limited number of members from the supporters club will be invited to a series of special events to be held from February 12 to February 14. If you wish to apply for membership, please visit the Web site at www.dartfordcityfc.com for further information.

| www.dartfordcityfc.com | | | |
|---|---|---|---|
| **Application for membership for the 2023 – 2024 season** | | | |
| I agree to the terms and conditions of the supporters club and would like to apply for an annual membership as below: | | | |
| Name: | *Floyd Williams* | Age: | *37* |
| Address | *291 St. Peter's Squire, Dartford* | Zip Code: | *WD1 2DE* |
| Phone number: | (Home) *391 – 0201* | (Mobile) *0883 - 00117* | |
| E-mail address: | *floydwilliams@tescoline.com* | | |
| Preferred Type of Membership: | | *Family* | |
| Comment: *I'd like to attend the event to be held on Day 2 with my twin children and am wondering in which way our application should be made, together or separately. I look forward to hearing from you soon.* | | | |

SEND

**21.** Who was Mr. McGregor in 2015?

(A) A city official

(B) A mayor

(C) A club supporter

(D) A business owner

**22.** What is true about the previous stadium?

(A) It did not have a press conference room.

(B) It caused a problem for the team to be promoted.

(C) It was located far from the shopping mall.

(D) It seated one hundred thousand spectators.

**23.** When does Mr. Williams want to join the event?

(A) On February 11

(B) On February 12

(C) On February 13

(D) On February 14

**24.** Who will most likely attend the opening ceremony?

(A) Floyd Williams

(B) Sean McGregor

(C) Arthur Reed

(D) Geoff Moore

**25.** What is implied about Dartford City Football Club?

(A) It has been sponsored by local companies.

(B) It suffered from some financial problems.

(C) It has a plan to renovate the stadium.

(D) It achieved good results several years ago.

## Vocabulary Check!

Choose an appropriate translation for the following words.  🔊 61

| | | |
|---|---|---|
| **1.** intensive ( ) | **2.** receptionist ( ) | **3.** refurbishment ( ) |
| **4.** pharmacy ( ) | **5.** ambulance ( ) | **6.** draft ( ) |
| **7.** nutritionist ( ) | **8.** emotionally ( ) | **9.** pedestrian ( ) |
| **10.** receipt ( ) | **11.** prescription ( ) | **12.** demolish ( ) |

| | | | |
|---|---|---|---|
| a. 救急車 | b. 受付係 | c. 改装 | d. 草稿案 |
| e. 栄養士 | f. 集中した | g. 感情的に | h. 解体する |
| i. 歩行者 | j. 受領書 | k. 処方箋 | l. 薬局 |

## 🎧 Listening Section

### Part 1　Photographs

**Strategy for Part 1 ［写真描写問題の解き方］**

**人物 1 人の写真 ④**

　人物が 1 人だけ写っていて、その人物にフォーカスが当たっていても、性別が分からない場合、主語は He, She, A man, A woman だけでは表現できず、職業名、（A doctor, A receptionist, The teacher）で、その人物を表す選択肢も出現します。しかし、どの選択肢が正解なのかはもちろん主語だけでは判別せずに、文全体を聞いてから正解を選びましょう。

1.

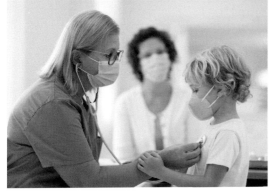

Ⓐ Ⓑ Ⓒ Ⓓ

2.  62

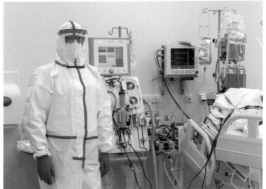

Ⓐ Ⓑ Ⓒ Ⓓ

### Part 2　Question-Response

**Strategy for Part 2 ［応答問題の解き方］**

**否定疑問文など ③　A か B か選ぶ選択疑問文**

　設問中に A or B という、「A か B か」の表現が入る選択疑問文は必然的に設問文が長くなり、難しく感じるかもしれませんが、答えのパターンを学習しておきましょう。正解のパターンとして「A のみ」「B のみ」「どちらでもよい」「どちらも不可」「まだ決まっていない」などがあります。

🔊 63

3.　Mark your answer on your answer sheet.　Ⓐ Ⓑ Ⓒ

4.　Mark your answer on your answer sheet.　Ⓐ Ⓑ Ⓒ

5.　Mark your answer on your answer sheet.　Ⓐ Ⓑ Ⓒ

6.　Mark your answer on your answer sheet.　Ⓐ Ⓑ Ⓒ

## Part 3 Conversations

**Strategy for Part 3 [会話問題の解き方]**

図表を含む問題 ③

　図表を含む問題では、図表を見ただけで正解できてしまっては、リスニングの問題になりません。必ず音声と図表の内容の両方から正解を導き出すようになっています。例えば図表の縦列に時間が並んでいて、別の縦列に固有名詞が並んでいる場合には、予定表や時刻表の可能性を考えて、図表に示してある時間や名詞が聞こえるのを待ち構えながら聞きましょう。

Questions 7-9

🔊 64

### Smiley Dental Clinic

| | Today's Clients | |
|---|---|---|
| | Dr. Cho | Dr. White |
| 9:30 AM | Staff Meeting | Mrs. Cambell |
| 11:00 AM | Staff Meeting | |
| Break Time | | |
| 2:00 PM | Mr. Smith | Mr. Thomas |
| 3:30 PM | | Mr. Bowors |

7. Why did the woman call the man?
   (A) She had her right arm injured.
   (B) She was late this morning.
   (C) She had to use a different road.
   (D) She wants to change an appointment.

8. What will Mr. Wrights do this afternoon?
   (A) Join a staff meeting
   (B) Have a business trip
   (C) See his client
   (D) Study abroad

9. Look at the graphic. Who will the man probably see today?
   (A) Dr. Cho
   (B) Dr. White
   (C) Mrs. Cambelt
   (D) Mr. Smith

## Part 4 Talks

Questions 10-12　🔊 65

**10.** Who most likely are the listeners?

(A) Pharmacists

(B) Nurses

(C) Computer experts

(D) Company executives

**11.** Where will Ms. Lindsey probably demonstrate?

(A) At a doctor's office

(B) At a pharmacy

(C) In a conference room

(D) In a company building

**12.** What are the listeners asked to do before the event?

(A) Contact an Internet provider

(B) Activate their computer

(C) Get familiar with the manual

(D) Confirm their password

## Part 5　Incomplete Sentences

### Strategy for Part 5 ［短文穴埋め問題の解き方］

**語彙問題 ①** 「不定詞」と「動名詞」の使い分け

☆**不定詞と動名詞を使い分ける問題**

　不定詞を目的語にとる語と、動名詞を目的語にとる語のどちらかを選ぶ場合には空所の後に何が続くかをみましょう。

「to 不定詞」だけを目的語にとる動詞には
　　want, hope, promise, agree, decide, mean, offer, wish など、
　　「～したい」「するつもりだ」の意味の動詞が多い。

「動名詞」だけを目的語にとる動詞には
　　enjoy, avoid, deny, mind, stop, consider, finish など、
　　「～し終える」「熟考する」「避ける」の意味が多い。

「to 不定詞」も「動名詞」も目的語にとる動詞には

| | | |
|---|---|---|
| remember | remember to 不定詞 | （忘れないで…する） |
| | remember ～ ing | （…したことを覚えている） |
| forget | forget to 不定詞 | （…するのを忘れる） |
| | forget ～ ing | （…したことを忘れる） |

などがあります。

13. It is important for the classified advertisement ------- the students' attention.
    (A) caught　　　　(B) catch　　　　(C) to catch　　　　(D) catches

14. I'm so sorry ------- you waiting so long in the lobby on such a cold day.
    (A) like　　　　(B) that　　　　(C) to make　　　　(D) to have kept

15. How nice ------- to give me such good advice.
    (A) of you　　　　(B) to you　　　　(C) for you　　　　(D) you that

16. Karen cannot expect ------- the first draft of the medical report by next week.
    (A) finish　　　　(B) finished　　　　(C) finishing　　　　(D) to finish

## Part 6  Text Completion

**Strategy for Part 6** ［長文穴埋め問題の解き方］

**必要な文法力 ②**

Unit 7 で紹介した Part 6 の「2. 文脈に沿って解く設問」のうち、**「動詞の形を選ぶ問題」**は、Part 6 全 16 問中、2 問程度出題されます。

例えば「過去形」「現在形」「未来表現」「現在完了形」の選択肢のうち、どれが空所に入るかを問われたとしましょう。

まず① **時制**、② **態** の 2 つの文法事項を理解しておき、（1）文法的に間違っている選択肢をはずします。すると、文法的に正しい選択肢が複数残ります。その上で（2）前後の文脈から時制を決めて、その複数の選択肢からさらに正解を選ぶわけです。Part 6 の設問は、皆さんの「文法力」と「読解力」を同時に鍛えてくれるのかもしれませんね。

Questions 17-20 refer to the following memo.

Nelson Hospital ------- its parking rules for staff members because the construction
 **17.**
of the new building is scheduled to start in May. The current staff car-park will be

used by construction vehicles instead. Fortunately, the factory next to us kindly

offered us some of its parking lots during the construction. Please use them -------
 **18.**
the old disused building has been demolished and replaced with the new parking

spaces. The General Affairs Department will issue tentative parking stickers, so

please be sure to put it on the front window of your car. -------. In that case, please
 **19.**
bring the receipt to the reception so that you can get -------.
 **20.**

**17.** (A) will be changed

(B) will change

(C) have changed

(D) is going to be changed

**18.** (A) until   (B) after   (C) meanwhile   (D) thereby

**19.** (A) It will obstruct the ambulances coming in and out.

(B) We have two other designated parking areas nearby.

(C) Alternatively, you can use any of the local paid car parks.

(D) If we find any cars parked along the entrance, the drivers will be fined.

**20.** (A) charged   (B) ticketed   (C) deducted   (D) reimbursed

「アビメ」からわかること

Unit 7 の Part 4 で紹介した**「ABILITIES MEASURED（通称：アビメ）」**という、TOEIC テスト結果の下段に載っている 10 本の棒グラフ（オンライン IP を除く）ですが、こちらが表す「より深い」内容やその見方について、公式にはほとんど説明されていません。

リーディングセクションに関するものは右半分の 5 本ですが、「語彙問題」を除く Part 7 が関係するのは上 3 本と見られます。上から 1 本目には、Unit 2 で紹介した「文書の目的・概要を問うタイプ」、2 本目には「文書の詳細情報を問うタイプ」「選択肢を文書と照らし合わせるタイプ」の正解数が含まれているようです。さらに 1 本目と 3 本目両方に「選択肢を文書と照らし合わせるタイプ」「書き手の意図を推測するタイプ」「文が入る位置を問うタイプ」の正解数が含まれているとも言われています。

ほかのパートも含め、この「アビメ」からはかなり具体的で有用な情報が得られます。TOEIC の結果について先生方にご相談する際は、ぜひこの紙を持っていきましょう。

Questions 21-25 refer to the following Web pages.

www.localmed.com/news/

### Special Feature about Our Town's Hospitals
### ~ Robertson Hospital ~
*By Vanessa Perkins*

Robertson Hospital announced that its new building will be opened on March 25. The new facility is based on their unique concept of fusing the latest medical treatment with traditional health care.

Having been established by three young doctors in 1955, the then small clinic became a renowned hospital. "Yes, we've now become a large and famous hospital in fact," says the director of Robertson Hospital, Terry Wells. "Meanwhile, we've been growing along with this town and we'll provide local people with top-level and unique medical care from now on."

Lisa Milton follows Dr. Wells, "since the town is blessed with beautiful nature, we've been thinking of ways to use it effectively in our medical practice, especially the many local hot springs." Being located by the Tate River, the new building is equipped with hot spring baths on its top floor. One of the baths is in the open-air so that the patients can enjoy a breathtaking view and de-stress.

Recently, the hospital also signed a contract with some local farmers, who will provide its patients with locally-grown organic vegetables. "We shouldn't forget our health is influenced by our diet," emphasizes the hospital nutritionist, Allison Brooks. "We aim to use not only vegetables but also all local resources, such as wood and water." In fact, rich groundwater from the mountains supplies most of the water for the hospital's everyday use.

The hospital will welcome visitors and observers to the new facilities from March 29. For those of you who are interested, please visit the hospital Web site for further information.

/www.robertsonhospital.com/

### Notice (updated on April 3)

We are pleased to announce that we have received far more visitors and observers than expected after the new facilities were opened. However, we are concerned that such a large number of them may disturb our inpatients. Also, welcoming and showing so many visitors around may prevent our staff from properly carrying out their day-to-day duties.

Considering the situation mentioned above, we now have to limit the number of visitors and observers to just five groups a day. Accordingly, a reservation is required to observe our new facilities from April 5. Please click the following button for your reservation.

**Reserve**

Thank you for your cooperation
The Director of Robertson Hospital

---

21. What is the main purpose of the first Web page?

    (A) To notify of a refurbishment

    (B) To promote the town

    (C) To announce a new project

    (D) To introduce a local institution

22. Who is Ms. Brooks?

    (A) A hospital staff member

    (B) A local farmer

    (C) A town official

    (D) A medical journalist

23. When can visitors enter the new building without booking?

    (A) On March 24

    (B) On March 27

    (C) On April 4

    (D) On April 7

24. What is most likely true about Robertson Hospital?

    (A) It often had over five groups of visitors a day after March 29.

    (B) It is suffering from a shortage of skilled doctors.

    (C) Its main building was supposed to be relocated on April 3.

    (D) Its Web site is regularly updated by the director.

25. What is suggested about Ms. Milton?

    (A) She is one of the original staff members.

    (B) She is an assistant of the director.

    (C) She was interviewed along with Mr. Wells.

    (D) She was promoted to secretary-general.

## Vocabulary Check!

Choose an appropriate translation for the following words.

🔊 66

| | | |
|---|---|---|
| 1. proofread ( ) | 2. candidate ( ) | 3. greet ( ) |
| 4. overtime ( ) | 5. suitable ( ) | 6. industry ( ) |
| 7. evaluate ( ) | 8. detail ( ) | 9. rough ( ) |
| 10. standpoint ( ) | 11. supplemental ( ) | 12. meanwhile ( ) |

| | | | |
|---|---|---|---|
| a. 評価する | b. 粗い | c. 補足の | d. その間 |
| e. 立ち位置 | f. 詳細 | g. 校正する | h. 挨拶する |
| i. 超過勤務 | j. 産業 | k. 適した | l. 志願者 |

## 🎧 Listening Section

### Part 1　Photographs

**Strategy for Part 1** ［写真描写問題の解き方］

**写真問題のコツ ③**

　Part 1 では、put on と wear の識別問題が頻出します。今、身につけている動作を写真で表すことは難しいので、put on は間違いであることが多く、現在着ている状態を表す wearing を含む表現は比較的、正解の可能性が高くなります。

**1.**

Ⓐ Ⓑ Ⓒ Ⓓ

**2.**　🔊 67

Ⓐ Ⓑ Ⓒ Ⓓ

### Part 2　Question-Response

**Strategy for Part 2** ［応答問題の解き方］

**平叙文に答える問題**

　設問が疑問文の形をしていない「平叙文」のパターンは聞き取りポイントを絞ることができませんが、「会話の流れ」をとらえることが一番大切です。

🔊 68

**3.**　Mark your answer on your answer sheet.　　Ⓐ Ⓑ Ⓒ

**4.**　Mark your answer on your answer sheet.　　Ⓐ Ⓑ Ⓒ

**5.**　Mark your answer on your answer sheet.　　Ⓐ Ⓑ Ⓒ

**6.**　Mark your answer on your answer sheet.　　Ⓐ Ⓑ Ⓒ

**Strategy for Part 3** ［会話問題の解き方］

図表を含む問題 ④

Part 3 では「～と言ったとき、どんな意味で言いましたか」という、意図を問う問題が出題されますが、その発言が聞こえたときにはすでに意図に関する情報は流れた後であることが多いです。音声の最初から状況を理解して聞く必要があります。

Questions 7-9　🔊 69

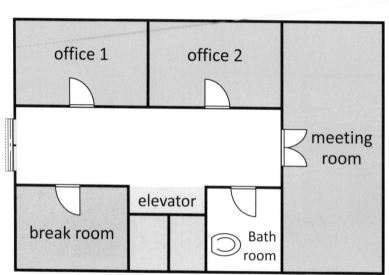

7.  Who is the man probably talking to?
    (A) A chef
    (B) A vice president
    (C) A mechanic
    (D) A receptionist

8.  Look at the graphic. Where does the man go for the interview?
    (A) The meeting room
    (B) Office 1
    (C) Office 2
    (D) The break room

9.  Why did the woman say, "The vice president is having lunch now"?
    (A) To tell him he has some time to spare
    (B) To tell him about the cafeteria
    (C) To emphasize the company atmosphere
    (D) To provide feedback on his résumé

## Part 4 ▸ Talks

Questions 10-12　　🔊 70

**10.** Which department does the speaker most likely work in?

(A) Sales

(B) Marketing

(C) General affairs

(D) Human resources

**11.** What did the management decide to do yesterday?

(A) To merge with another company

(B) To withdraw from the market

(C) To hire some new staff

(D) To open another branch

**12.** What are the listeners asked to do if possible?

(A) Apply for the positions

(B) Submit a list of applicants

(C) Check the job advertisement

(D) Contact their acquaintances

## **Part 5** Incomplete Sentences

---

**Strategy for Part 5** ［短文穴埋め問題の解き方］

**語彙問題 ②　単語の意味と文脈、前置詞との相性**

　語彙問題では基本的に文脈を理解して正解を特定します。しかし、それぞれの品詞の性質によって、結びつきの強い単語との相性を考えることで、文脈を理解するプロセスを短縮することができます。つまり、ほかの単語との相性から正解を導き出すことで、文全体を読まなくても解答することができるのです。

**☆動詞と前置詞との相性を覚えておこう**

　前置詞の問題には Unit 6 で説明した接続詞との使い分けのほかに、動詞とセットでの用法を問うものが多く語彙問題として出題されます。

・基本の前置詞：at「点のイメージ」、on「接触のイメージ」、in「包含のイメージ」
・自動詞とセットで使う例

| | |
|---|---|
| accuse（人）of … | （人を…のことで責める） |
| belong to … | （…に所属する） |
| deal with … | （…を扱う） |
| participate in … | （…に参加する） |

---

**13.** His wife could not prevent Jim ------- drinking alcohol at the dinner party.

(A) to (B) for (C) from (D) with

**14.** The price of travel to the interview rose ------- six dollars when I used a taxi.

(A) by (B) into (C) between (D) higher

**15.** The Buxton enterprise ------- 9 several departments with approximately 25,000 employees.

(A) consists by (B) consists of (C) is consist in (D) is consist out

**16.** If you have any questions ------- the promotion system, please consult Mr. Jenkins in the human resources department.

(A) regarding (B) regarded (C) regards (D) with regard

## Part 6　Text Completion

Questions 17-20 refer to the following job advertisement.

Erikson Travel Corporation is seeking someone suitable for the position of head manager of its new branch office. ------- the current fierce competition in the tourism
**17.**
industry, we will be opening a new office in Queen's Square. Applicants are required to have a degree in business administration, over three-years ------- experience
**18.**
and fluency in both French and Spanish languages. -------. If you would like to apply
**19.**
for the position, please send your résumé, two letters of ------- and certificates of
**20.**
your language skills to the personnel department at the following e-mail address: personnel@eriksontravel.co.uk. no later than 15 September. Successful candidates will be contacted by phone so that we can schedule an online interview.

**17.** (A) Facing　　(B) Faced　　(C) Having faced　　(D) It being faced

**18.** (A) manager　　(B) manage　　(C) manageable　　(D) managerial

**19.** (A) Also, familiarity with the tourism industry is preferred.
　　(B) Moreover, your travel expenses will be covered by the company.
　　(C) The details of the employee benefits will not be changed.
　　(D) They will be finalized by the board of directors soon.

**20.** (A) supervisor　　(B) predecessor　　(C) reference　　(D) compliance

| Strategy for Part 7 ［読解問題の解き方］ |
| --- |

**Reading・解く順番**

　皆さんは TOEIC L&R テストの際、リーディングセクションの各 part をどのような順に解いていますか。また、この順番について考えたことはありますか。

　リスニングセクションでは解答する順番を変えることはできませんが、リーディングセクションでは可能です。また Part 7 には、やはり 55 分程度は必要です。そこで、もし現在 Part 5 – 6 – 7 と順に解いていて時間が足りず、「もう少し時間があればもっと解けるのに」と感じている方には、「Part 5 – 7 – 6」という順番をお勧めします。そのように感じる方は特に、Part 7 に時間をかければ正解数が増えるからです。ちなみに Part 5 や Part 6 にかける時間を増やしても、あまり正解数は増えません。「知っていれば解けるし、知らなければ解けない」設問が多いからです。

　**「リーディングセクション全体でどのように正解数を増やすか」**という視点でよく考え、テスト本番前の**準備段階で、自分に最も向いている解き方を見つけておくとよいでしょう。**

Questions 21-25 refer to the following e-mails and contract.

| To: | Todd Harris <t.harris@ecosolutions.co.au> |
| --- | --- |
| From: | Natalie Melton <n.melton@ecosolutions.co.au> |
| Date: | 23 October |
| Subject: | Request for proofreading |
| Attachment: | My draft for the contract |

Dear Todd,

Thank you very much for joining us in the Human Resources department to interview James Lewis yesterday. Your comments and suggestions from a global business standpoint very much helped us decide to hire him. As you pointed out at the meeting after the interview, Mr. Lewis has not only outstanding management skills but also a clear-cut insight into the future of the environmental industry. That is one of the main reasons we decided to offer him the position of director and we believe he is someone who can help the company find its way in the market.

Please find attached my first draft for the written contract of employment with Mr. Lewis. I would appreciate it if you could check the details and give me some feedback by next Thursday. Please note that it is just a rough draft and there will be some supplements and further details for each of the articles.

Regards,
Natalie

## Employment Contract

Ecosolutions Co., Ltd. (the "Company") and James Lewis (the "Employee") hereby enter into the following contract of employment.

[...]

4. Responsibilities and Job Description
   Manage the marketing department, observe the ongoing overseas operations, evaluate new plans by the other departments, and advise the overseas subsidiaries and affiliated companies.

5. Work Hours
   Flextime, eight hours between 8:00 A.M. to 7:00 P.M. per day.

6. Holidays
   Holidays include Saturdays, Sundays, national holidays, from 23 December to 26 December, and summer holidays (seven days during the months of July and August).

7. Overtime Work
   Applicable

[...]

| To: | Natalie Melton <n.melton@ecosolutions.co.au> |
|---|---|
| From: | Todd Harris <t.harris@ecosolutions.co.au> |
| Date: | 25 October |
| Subject: | Re: Request for proofreading |

Dear Natalie,

Hello. I am writing to you to give you my suggestions as follows:

1) Mr. Lewis will have to attend the monthly online meeting of board directors as an advisor. I would suggest including it in his responsibilities.

2)  In Asia-based companies, most people do not take any days off in late December other than the new-year holidays. Why don't you ask him if he can take his holiday from 29 December to 3 January instead?

3)  Since our rules of regulation were revised last month, we have to be careful about his overtime hours. You might want to ask our legal department for their opinion.

I'll also be happy to check the supplemental documents if necessary.

Regards,
Todd

21. In which department does Mr. Harris most likely work?
    (A) Legal
    (B) Human Resources
    (C) International
    (D) Public Relations

22. In the second e-mail, which article does Mr. Harris NOT mention?
    (A) Article 4
    (B) Article 5
    (C) Article 6
    (D) Article 7

23. What will probably happen to the attachment soon?
    (A) It will be forwarded to the marketing department.
    (B) It will be uploaded to the Web site.
    (C) The Employee will make comments on it.
    (D) There will be some changes to it.

24. What will Ms. Melton most likely do next?
    (A) Send Mr. Harris her drafts for additional documents
    (B) Request her colleague to interview Mr. Lewis
    (C) Submit the draft to her immediate supervisor
    (D) Schedule another online meeting with Mr. Harris

25. What is suggested about the Employee?
    (A) He will attend the meeting of company executives.
    (B) He will be supervising the Human Resources department.
    (C) He has experience working in other countries.
    (D) He speaks multiple Asian languages.

# UNIT **15** Mini Test

**Part 1** Photographs

1.                                                                          🔊)) 71

Ⓐ Ⓑ Ⓒ Ⓓ

2.

Ⓐ Ⓑ Ⓒ Ⓓ

**3.**

Ⓐ Ⓑ Ⓒ Ⓓ

**4.**

Ⓐ Ⓑ Ⓒ Ⓓ

**Part 2** Question-Response

5. Mark your answer on your answer sheet.  Ⓐ Ⓑ Ⓒ  🔊 72

6. Mark your answer on your answer sheet.  Ⓐ Ⓑ Ⓒ

7. Mark your answer on your answer sheet.  Ⓐ Ⓑ Ⓒ

8. Mark your answer on your answer sheet.  Ⓐ Ⓑ Ⓒ

9. Mark your answer on your answer sheet.  Ⓐ Ⓑ Ⓒ

10. Mark your answer on your answer sheet.  Ⓐ Ⓑ Ⓒ  🔊 73

11. Mark your answer on your answer sheet.  Ⓐ Ⓑ Ⓒ

12. Mark your answer on your answer sheet.  Ⓐ Ⓑ Ⓒ

13. Mark your answer on your answer sheet.  Ⓐ Ⓑ Ⓒ

14. Mark your answer on your answer sheet.  Ⓐ Ⓑ Ⓒ

## Part 3  Conversations

Questions 15-17                                                        🔊 74

**15.** What problem is the man calling about?
   (A) A document is missing.
   (B) An organ is not functioning well.
   (C) The photocopier is not working.
   (D) The sound of the alarm is loud.

**16.** What does the woman say she'll do?
   (A) She'll remind the office staff about the problem.
   (B) She'll use the special functions.
   (C) She'll lead the workshop.
   (D) She'll visit the man's office.

**17.** What did the man mean when he said "Luckily, we have two other copy machines to use on the third and the fifth floor of the building"?
   (A) His coworkers will not use the broken machine.
   (B) He doesn't need to use the elevator.
   (C) There's plenty of paper.
   (D) The inspection won't cost much.

## Part 4  Talks

Questions 18-20                                                        🔊 75

**18.** What is the main purpose of the talk?
   (A) To provide instructions
   (B) To explain about the products
   (C) To describe the job
   (D) To recruit employees

**19.** What are the listeners advised not to do during the tour?

(A) Talk to the researchers

(B) Take photographs

(C) Touch the equipment

(D) Leave the group

**20.** What will most likely be provided for the listeners?

(A) Some documents

(B) Some food

(C) An ID tag

(D) A smart card

## 📖 Reading Section

### Part 5 · Incomplete Sentences

**21.** I'd like to be an interpreter, so ------- I could speak English as fluently as you.

(A) I should     (B) I wish     (C) I want     (D) I better

**22.** ------- the grocery store is closed on weekday evenings, the main shop will remain open 24 hours a day.

(A) Even though    (B) In summary    (C) Knew    (D) Have known

**23.** Don't worry about what people say about your test results. Let it ------- for a while.

(A) forget     (B) forgotten     (C) be forgotten     (D) to be forgotten

**24.** Yesterday my mother asked me if I would go shopping with her -------.

(A) yesterday

(B) the following day

(C) two days ago

(D) the previous day

**25.** If the bus had left on schedule, the team members ------- in Boston by now.

(A) arrived

(B) are arrived

(C) have arrived

(D) would have arrived

**26.** For more ------- on travel map, call the general office on the second floor.

(A) interest     (B) smaller     (C) information     (D) than information

## Part 6   Text Completion

Questions 27-30 refer to the following advertisement.

---

### Dolton University Launches its Online Education Program Soon

Do you want to study at university after work ------- taking a long trip to campus?
**27.**
Dolton University will be starting its online education program in September just
for you. A variety of courses will be available and can even be accessed on your
smart phone. Amazingly, most of the courses ------- live! This means that the classes
**28.**
will be provided to the university students on campus at the same time. Even more
surprisingly, the latest sound technology enables us to make you feel ------- you
**29.**
were in the classroom. Please visit our Web site to experience a free trial lecture
now. If you like it, please complete your online application by 31 August. -------. For
**30.**
more finance options, please contact the Admission Office at admission@dolton.
ac.ie.

---

27. (A) thereby       (B) while        (C) on            (D) without

28. (A) are streaming
    (B) will be streamed
    (C) streaming
    (D) have been streamed

29. (A) even though    (B) as if         (C) the same      (D) likewise

30. (A) The number of computers available is very limited.
    (B) The application process has not been fixed yet.
    (C) The list of course contents will be available after that.
    (D) The tuition can be paid by credit card.

Questions 31-35 refer to the following schedule and e-mails.

## Schedule for the Internship Orientation
## (as of September 3)

| 9:00 ~ | Opening Remarks | Hannah Austin, Director of the Human Resources Department |
|---|---|---|
| 9:10 ~ | Ice-breaking Session | (all the interns) |
| 10:30 ~ | Factory Tour | Mark Jennings, Plant Manager |
| 11:50 ~ | Outdoor Lunch | (Barbeque party in groups) |
| 13:00 ~ | Computer Workshop | Elena Grant, IT Department |
| 14:40 ~ | Meeting with the Directors | (interns from groups according to their departments) |

| To: | Human Resources Department <hr-dpt@willfood.com> |
|---|---|
| From: | Hannah Austin <h.austin@willfood.com> |
| Date: | September 9 |
| Subject: | Tomorrow's Orientation |

Dear all,

According to the weather forecast, we will have inclement weather tomorrow. Considering the situation, we may have to make some changes to the intern's orientation schedule.

First, transportation delays and cancelations are highly likely, especially early in the morning. Accordingly, it is expected that some of the interns who commute by train or bus probably won't be able to attend the first morning session. Why don't we cancel my opening remarks and the ice-breaking session and delay the starting time of the orientation to 10:30 A.M.? Also, since they will have to walk outdoors in some parts of the factory tour, I'll ask the plant manager if it can be rescheduled for the afternoon.

Next, I don't think we can enjoy the outdoor lunch party in the garden tomorrow. It is regrettable to cancel it, but what do you all think about having an indoor party in the cafeteria instead? If you agree, I was wondering if any of you could choose a good caterer, which can handle our urgent request, and order catering for 30 people.

Additionally, having suddenly accepted three more interns yesterday, we will need some additional laptops in tomorrow's workshop. Someone from the IT Department is supposed to take care of it. Could any of you send them a reminder, please?

I hope my flight won't be canceled this evening so that I can get home within today.

Please take care,
Hannah

| To: | Greg Hoffman <g.hoffman@willfood.com> |
| From: | Elena Grant <e.grant@willfood.com> |
| Date: | September 10 |
| Subject: | Today's Orientation |

Dear Greg,

I hope you managed to drive to the company safe and sound this morning.

We in the IT department were informed yesterday evening that the factory tour had been switched for the computer workshop. We were supposed to get some laptops ready in advance but our periodic security maintenance for the spare computers hasn't been completed yet. Therefore, we will hold the workshop in Computer Room One instead.

It is very good to hear that you found a caterer and chose the menu because we all know you are familiar with some of the best restaurants in town. I will see you later at the welcoming luncheon.

Have a good day,
Elena

**31.** What is the purpose of the first e-mail?

(A) To confirm the revised plan

(B) To inform of the additional sessions

(C) To suggest some schedule changes

(D) To update the participants about the event

**32.** When will the tour start?

(A) At 9:10 A.M.

(B) At 10:30 A.M.

(C) At 1:00 P.M.

(D) At 2:40 P.M.

**33.** What is implied about Mr. Hoffman?

(A) He belongs to the same department as Ms. Grant.

(B) He reminded Mr. Jennings of the schedule.

(C) He placed an order for the catering.

(D) He commutes to the company by train.

**34.** Which event will be most likely held at its original venue?

(A) The Ice-breaking Session

(B) The Outdoor Lunch

(C) The Computer Workshop

(D) The Meeting with the Directors

**35.** What is NOT suggested about Ms. Grant?

(A) She will be present in the computer room.

(B) She directly contacted Ms. Austin.

(C) She will meet the interns at lunch.

(D) She switched her turn with Mr. Jennings.

著 者

松本恵美子（まつもと えみこ）順天堂大学講師

西井賢太郎（にしい けんたろう）多摩大学グローバルスタディーズ学部専任講師

Sam Little（サム・リトル）

600点を目指す TOEIC® L&R TEST 演習

2023 年 2 月 20 日　　第 1 版発行
2024 年 3 月 20 日　　第 4 版発行

著　者　　松本恵美子・西井賢太郎・Sam Little
発行者　　前田俊秀
発行所　　株式会社　三修社
　　　　　〒 150-0001 東京都渋谷区神宮前 2-2-22
　　　　　TEL 03-3405-4511　　FAX 03-3405-4522
　　　　　振替 00190-9-72758
　　　　　https://www.sanshusha.co.jp
　　　　　編集担当 三井るり子・伊藤宏実
印刷・製本　日経印刷株式会社

©2023 Printed in Japan ISBN978-4-384-33520-0 C1082
表紙デザイン―峯岸孝之
本文デザイン & DTP―Shibasaki Rie
準拠音声録音―ELEC
準拠音声製作―高速録音株式会社

**教科書準拠 CD 発売**

本書の準拠 CD をご希望の方は弊社までお問い合わせください。